The First Time

Finding Myself and Looking for Love on Reality TV

COLTON UNDERWOOD

GALLERY BOOKS

NEW YORK   LONDON   TORONTO   SYDNEY   NEW DELHI

Some of the names in this book have been changed. Even in anonymity, they are remembered with appreciation and affection.

Gallery Books
An Imprint of Simon & Schuster, Inc.
1230 Avenue of the Americas
New York, NY 10020

First Gallery Books hardcover edition March 2020

GALLERY BOOKS and colophon are registered trademarks of Simon & Schuster, Inc.

For information about special discounts for bulk purchases, please contact Simon & Schuster Special Sales at 1-866-506-1949 or business@simonandschuster.com.

The Simon & Schuster Speakers Bureau can bring authors to your live event. For more information or to book an event, contact the Simon & Schuster Speakers Bureau at 1-866-248-3049 or visit our website at www.simonspeakers.com.

Interior design by Erika Genova

Manufactured in the United States of America

10 9 8 7 6 5 4 3 2 1

Library of Congress Cataloging-in-Publication Data

Names: Underwood, Colton, author.
Title: The first time : finding myself and looking for love on reality TV / Colton Underwood.
Description: First Gallery Books hardcover edition 2020 | New York : Gallery Books, 2020.
Identifiers: LCCN 2019054436 (print) | LCCN 2019054437 (ebook) | ISBN 9781982139384 (hardcover) | ISBN 9781982139391 (trade paperback) | ISBN 9781982139407 (ebook)
Subjects: LCSH: Underwood, Colton. | Television personalities--United States--Biography. | Bachelor (Television program)
Classification: LCC PN1992.4.U56 A3 2020 (print) | LCC PN1992.4.U56 (ebook) | DDC 791.4502/8092 [B]--dc23
LC record available at https://lccn.loc.gov/2019054436
LC ebook record available at https://lccn.loc.gov/2019054437

ISBN 978-1-9821-3938-4
ISBN 978-1-9821-3940-7 (ebook)

For my family and friends;
my girlfriend
and her family and friends;
and
Bachelor Nation!
When you asked,
I said yes!

Love you all
and
thank you.

"Whatever you do, don't pick a girl from Southern California."

—A friend

". . . but I don't know."

—Cassie Randolph

Contents

Author's Note

I fell in love on TV in front of millions of people. It is not something I planned or expected to happen. Love is not something you can plan. I see you nodding in agreement. I suspect we're like-minded in this regard. You believe in the magic of love, as I do, whether you're reading a romance or living one. With this book, I have written the romance I am currently living and loving, and I'm hoping it becomes my happily ever after. I am thrilled where I am now, but it's complicated. I still have a lot to learn and discover and a lifetime ahead of me. I would like people to realize, as I have, that it's okay not to have yourself all figured out. It's okay not to have all the answers. It's okay to ask, "Who am I? What do I want?" It's okay to laugh and cry and step boldly into the unknown and occasionally jump over a fence. It's okay to share your heart and show your vulnerability. This is the only way I know to live . . . and to love.

The Short List

On *The Bachelor*, I didn't have as much time to get to know someone as I might have wanted or thought I was going to get. In that sense, the show was like real life. Moments came and went in the blink of an eye. I promise you that won't happen here. To get us started, here are ten basic but essential facts about me.

1. I prefer texts over email, but it's best just to call me. You can spend all day texting what you can accomplish in a five-minute call.

2. I'm into country music now. But growing up I was Team *NSYNC over Team Backstreet Boys.

3. Brussels sprouts are my favorite food. I wonder what that says about me. A little weird, I suppose. Sushi is a close second.

4. Sangria is my favorite drink. If it's not on the menu, I'll have a glass of white wine.

5. I don't wash my blue jeans. Denim shrinks, and a good pair of blue jeans should be worshipped, not washed.

6. I wear shorts to bed if I'm sleeping with my dog. I don't wear anything if I'm alone.

7. I am a neat freak. Cass says I'm the messiest neat person she's ever met.

8. I prefer baths over showers. But I always shower before taking a bath.

9. Of the one thousand plus photos on my Instagram, my favorite is the picture of me and Cass right after *The Bachelor* finale. I could finally show everybody that I was with this incredible person who filled my heart with happiness.

10. Am I still a virgin? That's a big part of this book, so you're going to have to keep reading to learn the rest of the story. And no skipping ahead. If you do, you'll miss the next chapter, which—spoiler alert—reveals something heretofore known only to Cass and me.

PART ONE

What's Your Number?

How Do You Not Know by Now?

I was standing on the dock, the turquoise water behind me, and my eyes were glued to the spot where Cassie would be arriving. I was eager to see her. I knew she would look great, all cute and sexy. I imagined staring into her eyes and seeing her smile up close and touching her soft, warm skin. I was still trying to figure out my life, but this much I knew for sure: being with Cassie made me happy.

It was week five of *The Bachelor*. We were newly arrived in Thailand after a week in Singapore, and I was waiting for my first one-on-one date with Cassie Randolph, a twenty-three-year-old blond from Huntington Beach, California. She had occupied my thoughts for days. Intrigued. Smitten. A little obsessed. Maybe more than a little. Call it what you want. I knew I was supposed to be open-minded, but Cassie was the girl I wanted to spend time with more than any of the others, and when producers informed me to get ready for a one-on-one with her, my smile expressed a well of pent-up excitement that literally rose from my toes all the way to the top of my head and exploded from me in a single word: *Finally!*

I was sure they already sensed my interest in her. Same with Cass. The two of us felt the initial blush of attraction when we first said hello, and since then I'd managed to sneak in several conversations with Cass that confirmed the fact. The producers picked up on the vibe but moved slowly and cautiously. They knew that Cass was reserved and careful about opening up emotionally, and they wanted her to get more comfortable with me before we were on our first one-on-one date.

They were right.

Everything about this date was perfect—except the weather.

We were supposed to go snorkeling. I couldn't have picked a better activity for a first date. I love the water. I grew up snorkeling and scuba diving with my family. I was skilled and confident in my ability. Since Cassie lived in a beach community and her little brother was a serious surfer, I figured she enjoyed water sports, too. As a bonus, both of us would be in swimsuits. The date was going to be fun—really fun.

The anticipation made me impatient as I watched the crew load the dive boat and block their camera positions. I'm not good at waiting around for something to happen, good or bad. Stray dogs milled around the dock. They were everywhere in Thailand. A couple of them sniffed at my feet, trying to make friends, hoping I had food. I resisted the urge to pet them. I didn't want to get stray-dog scent on me before the date.

Then the van bringing Cassie arrived. After the crew checked their shot with producers, the door opened and there she was. Perfectly framed: blond and smiling. She got out and joined me on the dock. She wore a black bathing suit top and white-and-tan-striped culottes and looked super cute. She would've looked super cute in anything.

She was eager to learn about our date. I teased the plans without revealing specific details, as was my role as the Bachelor. The details had changed only a few minutes earlier. While waiting for Cassie, it had started to rain. Though the rain was light and felt pleasant in the thick, humid air, it made shooting underwater impossible. So producers scratched the scuba diving and instead

Cass and I were headed to a small sandbar—a private island, in *Bachelor* parlance—where we could frolic in tropical isolation.

"Let's get out of here," I said, helping Cassie on board.

As the boat started up and skimmed over the clear blue water, we cuddled up next to each other and talked until the island came into view. Cassie laughed, clearly delighted with this postage-stamp-size paradise of our own. We jumped out and held hands as we ran onto the sand. Everything was warm—the water, the air, Cassie's skin.

Cassie and I turned toward each other at the same time. She was smiling—a good sign. We ran around, kicked at the water, and kissed (and kissed some more) before sitting down on a log in the middle of the sandbar to talk. We were eager to get to know each other. Aware that she was studying speech pathology, I told her that I struggled with a lisp when I was little and still had trouble with my *s*'s when I got anxious. She said she could help.

The producers had an uncanny ability to interrupt and pull us for interviews right when I wished none of them were there. *What do you think? What are you feeling? What do you like about her? Everything about her was perfect,* I thought. *The sound of her voice. Her laugh. Her eyes. The way she looks in that black bikini . . .*

Then Cassie and I were in the water again. The producers wanted a shot of us from above. They launched a drone. The boat pulled away from us, out of the picture. "Don't say anything personal or important," one of the producers warned. A second later Cass and I had the same realization. We weren't wearing microphones. No one was listening in on our conversation. We didn't have cameras pointed at us. Or crew members standing two feet away. It was a rarity on *The Bachelor.* We were alone.

In the warm ocean.

Holding each other.

Kissing.

I closed my eyes in order to savor everything about this gorgeous, playful, sensual moment. I wanted this imprinted in my memory forever. But when I opened my eyes again and gazed down at Cass, expecting to find a similarly romantic look in return, I saw instead a young woman who was looking up at me with an intensely serious curiosity.

"How do you not know by now?" she said.

She wasn't joking. There was no *ha-ha* or *wink-wink* in her expression. Her question was straight to the point, real, and stunningly revealing of a young woman with the character and courage to seize a rare opportunity and ask for the truth.

How do you not know by now?

I knew what she meant, but I wasn't prepared for the directness and honesty of her question. Basically, she wanted me to flip to the end of the book and tell her how the story ended. I couldn't. I didn't know myself.

"That's not a fair question," I said.

Cassie tilted her head to the side.

"You have all these beautiful women and you still don't know?" she said. "You have to know a little bit."

She might've been right. We were more than a month into the show, and, as I knew from my previous experiences on *The Bachelorette* and *Bachelor in Paradise*, there comes a time early on in this amorous adventure when sparks fly and the promise of something more compels further exploration or there's zero romantic connection and, well, those people are the first to get sent home. Cassie made my heart flutter and dance with curiosity and desire, and the fact that we had cameras pointed at us was beside the point. My emotions were real.

Very real.

And that's a scary thing. To expose those feelings and risk that hurt.

With millions of people watching.

Except you aren't thinking about them.

Cassie sure wasn't—and it told me so much about her. *How did I not know?* That would be the prism through which I looked at everyone for the remainder of the show. *How did I not know? What did I know?* Cassie must have been asking herself the same questions. All of us were. Everyone on the show. I had spent years thinking about love and falling in love and wondering who that person might be and how I would know when it happened. Was it possible I'd meet her on a reality TV show?

If I did, would she feel the same way? Would she know?

I held Cassie in my arms. I kissed her.

What if she didn't know?

How do we truly know about anything?

Only twenty-six years old at the time, I was trying to figure myself out and constantly asked myself such questions and more. Who was I? What should I do with my life? Perhaps identity and the search for it was a lifelong quest. As a little boy, I wondered what I wanted to do when I grew up. As a teenager, I wondered how I would know when I liked a girl and then how would I know when it was the right time to kiss her. Then came the question about sex. Actually, there were many questions about sex. Some I knew how to ask. Some I didn't. How would I know when it was the right time? And with whom? How would I know when I fell in love? How would I know it was the forever kind of love?

The one thing I knew about myself with absolute certainty was that I was sometimes confused.

And then there was Cassie.

How did I not know? How does anyone ever know?

A Promise Broken

"I'm sorry, I shouldn't have asked that."

Cassie was staring straight into my eyes for some sign of assurance, and I had to quickly turn away before I told her too much. We were back on the boat, but not yet wearing microphones. The crew was still getting themselves situated. When I didn't immediately respond, she apologized again. I put my hand on her knee and told her an apology wasn't necessary. It was okay, I said. I understood. I truly did.

Cassie was simply being real, which wasn't simple at all. From having been in a similar position as she was now, I knew she wanted some kind of assurance from me that we were on the same page. At the very least, that I had narrowed down my interest to two or three girls and that she was among them. Even that was scary. Who wants to compete for affection? Her heart must have been in her throat. Her feelings were genuine, and being aware of the cameras surrounding her, she was only protecting herself before she exposed any real feelings and made herself vulnerable, open to scrutiny and possible pain.

On the island, I told her that I didn't like playing games. How could I look into her eyes and say anything without sounding disingenuous?

Then again, we were, in fact, playing a game. *The Bachelor*, like its prime-time siblings, *The Bachelorette* and *Bachelor in Paradise*, was a dating experiment on steroids. It was Bumble, OkCupid, Tinder, and Match.com all mashed together times one hundred. I loved the show. I was addicted and freaked out at the same time. The goal was to find the person you wanted to be with forever. From my first time as a participant, I alternated between excitement and fear, often wondering if I could separate the two emotions. It was the same thing Cassie was experiencing. In matters of the heart, excitement and fear were two sides of the same coin. I knew when the feelings weren't there. And when they were there? Why was it such a mess? Why were there always so many questions?

Was it really love?

Would it last? How could I be sure?

How did I not know?

I knew the poet's famous line about love, but was it really better to have loved and lost?

I hated to lose. I was still nursing a broken heart after getting dumped a year earlier from my first serious relationship. How long was that injury supposed to last? My broken shoulder healed faster. When I loved, I was all in. I opened my heart as wide as possible, and the bruises from that breakup were still raw, tender, and painful to touch. I'm sensitive, perhaps overly and unexpectedly so.

You don't have to be Dr. Freud to find the root cause of that condition. Like a lot of people my age, I still bore the scars of my parents' divorce even though both of them had remarried and I loved my blended family of bonus parents and siblings as much as you can love anyone in your family. But my parents' split was a jarring hit. As with those ferocious hits on the football field that come out of nowhere, it was hard to get up after that one.

Don't get me wrong. As I said a moment ago, I love my parents, Donna and Scott. They're Mom and Dad, and they're also my best friends. I still finish our phone calls by saying, "Bye, I love you." But

I'm like a lot of kids who had a hard time seeing their parents as individuals separate from Mom and Dad, with problems and issues they were trying to figure out. They were college sweethearts and star athletes at Illinois State University (ISU). Mom was all-state in volleyball and Dad was an all-state defensive lineman on the football team.

After graduation they married and moved to Indianapolis, Indiana. Within a year, they started a family. I was born January 26, 1992. My brother, Connor, arrived eighteen months later. Mom and Dad were thrilled. When I was six years old, we moved to Washington, Illinois, the small town where my dad had grown up and still enjoyed notoriety as a local football hero. We moved into an eight-thousand-square-foot, seven-bedroom home that felt too big for our tiny family. I once caught a bat in the attic and took it to school for show-and-tell.

As Dad grew his construction business, he inherited a twenty-acre plot of land and began turning it into a family compound, with homes for us, his parents, and his two sisters. Once construction began, he sold our large house and we moved into a condominium. A year later, our new house was ready. When the concrete floor was poured in the garage, my mom and dad and Connor and I all put our handprints in the corner. I assumed they'd be there forever, and so would we.

My grandparents moved into their house. Then one of my aunts moved into her house. I remember the comfort I got from running over to my grandparents' house one day when we ran out of milk. I was surrounded by family. I was related to everyone on my block. We vacationed as a group, too. Every year on my brother's birthday, in July, we went to Lake Shelbyville with my mom's parents and her brother's family. As I got older, we added an annual vacation to Mexico or some other warm-weather spot.

My brother and I had tractors, ATVs, and go-carts. We had a big swimming pool and a pond where we fished. One summer we set up a huge Slip 'N Slide down the hill and into the water that was like the coolest thing I could ever imagine. You get the picture. It was a paradise for boys.

When I was in fourth grade, I started playing Pop Warner football. Given my dad's background, putting on a helmet and pads was inevitable. Connor joined the team the next year. We were the Washington Panthers. I was a big kid and strong, but also overweight, goofy, and awkward. I played center and defensive line, the positions that went to the larger kids. I learned to block, tackle, and just take up a lot of space.

My dad coached the team and saw to it that my brother and I worked harder than anyone else. Even at this junior level, he pushed us hard, often harder than anyone else, as he expected and wanted much more from the two of us. When I hit my limit, though, I always did the same thing. I threw down my helmet, announced that I was quitting, and stormed off the field. My dad never said a word. Never chased me. He waited until I turned around, walked back, and said, "Okay, I'll play."

In the sixth grade, I made my school's basketball team. It was the first time I made a team that one of my parents didn't coach and the highlight of my athletic career up to that point. I helped the team into the regionals, where we won a few games before getting knocked out of the tournament. I continued to play in seventh and eighth grade, but there was never a question which sport would be my number one when I got to high school.

In addition to having been an all-state legend at Washington High, my dad coached the high school's freshman team and was a varsity assistant. As such, I had a reputation before I even got there. But it was a good one. I had grown and started to slim down. I was still pudgy, but that fat was turning to muscle from the hours I spent lifting weights and hoping to one day turn pro like my idols Michael Strahan, Dwight Freeney, and Peyton Manning.

Three weeks before the summer workouts my freshman year, I nearly blew it. I jammed my foot into a door while playing hide-and-seek with friends and broke my toe. It swelled up and turned black and blue immediately. I knew it was bad.

I kept the injury to myself and went to football camp as if nothing was wrong. I fought through pain that worsened with each drill and thought I'd impressed the varsity's head coach, Darrell Crouch, as well as my dad. At the end of the day, though, Coach Crouch whistled me over to the side.

"What's up with your foot?" he said. "You're limping."

"Yeah, it's nothing," I lied. "One of the lineman stepped on my toe. It might be broken. I don't know."

"Get it checked and taken care of," he said.

The team's doctor took one look and pronounced my toe broken without even taking an X-ray. I didn't tell him or anyone else how I actually broke it for the longest time. The last thing I wanted was for someone to think I was screwing around and not 100 percent dedicated to football. Despite missing the rest of the preseason practices and games, I made the freshman and sophomore teams *and* I was put on varsity, too. I was the only kid to get three jerseys.

There were cries of nepotism ("the dude hasn't even padded up" and "he only got this far because of his dad"), but once my toe healed, I started for both the varsity and sophomore teams at center on offense and lineman on defense. Then, midway through the season, the team's captain and all-area safety, Mike Minehan, and our quarterback, Austin Fisher, encouraged me to switch to fullback. They saw I was big, strong, and fast.

I thrived in the new position and also in playing both sides of the ball. In the last game of the season, I was on the field for every snap on both offense and defense for all three of our teams—freshman, sophomore, and varsity.

Such exploits didn't endear me to those in my own grade—and

looking back, I understand why some thought of me as bigheaded. They saw me hanging out with my teammates, all of whom were upperclassmen, and during games they saw me in an environment where I was aggressive and cocky. I think it made me seem arrogant when the opposite was true. I was shy, introverted, and more than a little insecure.

As it turned out, I was popular with college coaches. During my sophomore season, I received recruiting letters and inquiries from numerous schools. The list got longer the next year, and it was pretty obvious I could get a scholarship if I worked hard, which I did. I trained every day for two hours before school, signed up for a weight-lifting period, and then I went to practice after classes. Such discipline and another growth spurt turned me into an elite competitor who scored, tackled, and took charge on the field.

My best game of the year was against nearby Morton High. I was responsible for four touchdowns—I rushed for one, caught a ball in the end zone, threw for a TD, and ran back an interception. I was named Large-School Player of the Year. But the most meaningful accolade I received was in a write-up in the Peoria newspaper when our quarterback said, "[Colton's] such a big guy that he comes off as intimidating. But he's got one of the biggest hearts on the team. You can always go to him if you have a problem."

My dad guided me through the college process. Between my sophomore and junior years, we visited prospective schools so I could work out with their other recruits. At South Carolina, I ran with the offense. Then we went to University of Florida, whose legendary coach, Urban Meyer, had coached my dad at ISU. In my first drill, I went up against a dude who was my age and stood about six five and weighed more than three hundred pounds. As soon as the whistle blew, he stood me up, picked me up, and then slammed me to the ground.

Talk about a reality check. Back home, I was the one who put people on their backs. Not this time.

My dad saw the whole thing.

"You learned something, didn't you?" he said.

Three days later I squared off against the same guy. I didn't win, but I didn't get knocked on my ass, either. I got a little better and a little smarter. Which was the point of the trip. My dad had wanted to expose me to the level of talent beyond my high school, and it worked. After more bruising stops at Iowa, Wisconsin, and Illinois State, I went back to Washington, worked my butt off, and had the best season of my career.

Prior to my senior year, after considering a number of scholarship offers from schools around the Midwest, I made a verbal commitment to Illinois State University, my dad's alma mater. The school was only forty-five minutes from home, so my family would be able to get to the games easily and I would be able to come home whenever I wanted. ISU also offered me a spot on defense, which no other school did. I knew I wasn't going to make the NFL as a fullback. Defense was my shot—and I loved playing D.

On February 3, 2009—only a few days after my eighteenth birthday—I signed a national letter of intent in the school library surrounded by my family, my high school teammates and coaches, and ISU head coach Brock Spack and linebacker coach Spence Nowinsky. The local newspaper covered the event, and we celebrated at home with my favorite dinner—wiener roll-ups (mashed potatoes, a hot dog, and cheddar cheese baked in a Pillsbury crescent roll).

It didn't happen without a little drama. Earlier that morning, the University of Wisconsin had offered me a full-ride scholarship. Apparently they had lost their top prospect at fullback and knew I was still available, at least for the moment. The lure of Wisconsin was obvious to anyone familiar with college football. It was a Big Ten school, they played on national television, the exposure was huge, and they sent fullbacks into the NFL.

Just in case I was tempted, my dad sat me down and reminded me that I had been raised to honor my commitments. My word was my reputation.

"If you start something," he said.

"I know, I know," I interrupted. "I'm expected to finish it."

Although still in high school, I was eager to start learning the new system. One day I skipped school and drove to Illinois State to watch the team practice. Coach Nowinsky wrapped his arm around me in front of a couple of sophomores and juniors and gloated, "I can't wait for this motherfucker to come here, kick your ass, and take your spot." The guys weren't amused, and I arrived on campus the next summer a marked man.

During training camp, I tried too hard to prove myself. In scrimmages, I was all over the field. Coach Nowinsky told me to stop trying to make every play.

"This isn't high school," he said. "You aren't going to make every tackle here in college. We have other guys like you, with your ability. Just stay in your gap. Focus on your job."

The advice paid off. I was one of two freshmen who started. With sixteen tackles, I more than proved that I belonged. I might've done even better, but midway through the year the coaching assignments were shuffled and the linebackers were taken away from Coach Nowinsky and given to another coach, whom I didn't respond to well. I told Coach Nowinsky that I was unhappy and wanted to transfer if the situation didn't change.

"Everything's going to be okay," he said. "It'll be good next year."

And it was. After the season, the coach I disliked was fired, I was reunited with Coach Nowinsky, and I had my best season yet as a sophomore. I was credited with thirty-eight tackles and earned All-Missouri Valley Football Conference honorable mention. Pro teams scouted me. I was ready for my football career to take off in a big way. All my hard work seemed like it was going to pay off. I loved playing college football, and my dream of playing in the NFL seemed like it was just around the corner.

It was a helluva good time until, suddenly, it wasn't. One weekend, shortly after summer lifting had started prior to my junior year, I went home to hang out with my family, as I did nearly every weekend. I was more comfortable being with my parents, grandparents, and two black Labs, Sniper and Bullet, than I was with my three roommates, whose weekend pursuits were much more typical, in that they liked to drink, party, and chase girls. They teased me for being a straight arrow, but I wasn't comfortable being anything else.

I was a homebody. I really enjoyed chilling out at home with my family. I watched TV, ate, slept. Why was that a bad thing?

Anyway, my brother came home from Indiana State that same weekend. It was coincidental. The two of us were rarely home the same weekend during the school year. He was more like my roommates. The two of us were catching up and bullshitting in the kitchen when my parents walked in. I could tell something was wrong right away. Dad's eyes were red, and Mom looked as if she'd been crying. I braced myself for bad news. Someone was sick or something had gone wrong with Dad's business. Anything except what Dad said.

"Your mother and I are getting a divorce."

My mom simply nodded while Dad, in a soft, deliberate, serious tone of voice, continued to address Connor and me. His explanation offered very little detail other than their marriage was no longer working as they believed marriages should. They wanted each other to be happy, something they hadn't been for a long time. Connor and I shouldn't worry, he said, as my mother signaled her agreement. We would still be a family, and they would still be there for us, as they always had been.

I suppose my dad said all the right things. It's just that I didn't hear most of it. The second I heard the word *divorce*, it was like getting knocked down and out by a three-hundred-pound lineman and having everything look different when I finally regained consciousness. I thought of divorce as the ultimate failure. I saw the two people I loved more than anyone else walking away from the family I loved more than anything else. They were giving up on us, I thought. They were walking away from the family they had created. Sure, they might've had problems, I told myself, but what the fuck, fix them. Don't divorce.

What about the commitment you made to each other? To Connor and me?

They didn't enter into this decision lightly. It had been years in the making, I later learned. But there in the kitchen I didn't possess the emotional tools or maturity to ask even the most basic questions or to try to understand my parents as individuals who had their own complicated issues, just as I did. They probably needed a hug more than I did at that moment. I wish I would've had the wherewithal to listen to my dad, talk to both him and my mom, and see that they were in pain.

All I felt was anger—an anger that boiled and raged until it consumed me.

"I'm outta here," I said, hopping off the kitchen counter.

I flashed everyone a defiant look, like we were squaring off on the football field, before I stormed out of the house. I got in my Jeep and stepped on the gas with every ounce of strength I had in me. The tires bit into the pavement with a loud, primal screech that mirrored the way I felt inside. I ran at least two stop signs on my way back to school. I couldn't get away fast enough from the only place I'd ever wanted to be.

It's All Going to Be Okay

As a college junior, my efforts on the football field earned me all-American honors. I stood six feet three inches and weighed 265 pounds. I benched 465 pounds, squatted 605 pounds, and cleaned over 300 pounds. In shoulder pads and a helmet, I looked like a gladiator in armor. In my uniform, I was the picture of a hypermasculine strongman, the star player, an action hero. I tossed opponents to the side, made tackles, and sprang up from horrific pile-ups. I seemed like nothing could hurt me.

But the impression I gave on the field didn't reflect the emotions and vulnerabilities I struggled with off the field. The shock of my parents' divorce created new wounds and exposed old injuries I thought had gone away. I remembered the way I'd been bullied as a sixth grader at St. Patrick Catholic School. Every day a group of kids called me names like fatso and four lips and made fun of my speech impediment. I dreaded lunchtime and recess when I was alone on the playground. I begged my parents to let me transfer.

I would've never guessed that kind of pain would return all these years later. But in the weeks and months after my parents revealed they were splitting up, I walked around feeling confused and hurt and lost. My size and strength disguised the fact that I was still a kid, only nineteen, and in shock. Under normal circumstances

I would've asked my mom and dad for help with this problem the way I did when I wanted to change schools in sixth grade. They were my pillars. I depended on their strength and guidance.

They would've been available and willing to talk if I'd gone to them, but I tried to deal on my own. It wasn't the healthiest choice. I internalized everything. I was so angry, and then I felt disappointed and let down—and not just by my mom and dad. I questioned my faith in God. Though I no longer went to church regularly, I still believed in God—or wanted to. I didn't see any signs that things would get better no matter how hard I prayed. I remember saying, "Really, dude? You're going to let this happen in my life?"

One day, in the middle of football practice, I ran off the field feeling strange and anxious, like my heart was pounding triple time. When I got to the sideline, I bent down on one knee, feeling out of breath and a little out of control. I wasn't focused on football, I realized. My thoughts were racing. My dad had put our house up for sale. Both he and my mom were moving to Denver. They wanted a fresh start, he said, and they wanted to be close enough where they could still offer each other support. In retrospect, that was very cool of them. However, at the time, I just thought, *You're leaving? What about me?*

Coach Nowinsky ran over to where I was trying to catch my breath and squatted next to me. He looked into my eyes.

"You okay?" he asked. "What's going on?"

I told Coach that I needed to talk to him in private. After practice, we went into his office, and as soon as he shut the door and walked around to his side of the desk, I started to cry. I couldn't help it. The dam just burst. I told him what was going on with my family and explained I was shaken, confused, angry, and scared. I was also mad—not that he couldn't tell from all the f-bombs I dropped after I quit crying. I felt betrayed.

"What about everything he always told me about commitment?" I said.

"I know your folks," he said. "They're good people. The thing you come to realize as you grow up and get older is that your parents are people, too. They aren't infallible. They're trying to figure out their lives the same as everyone else."

A week later, Coach Nowinsky invited me to have dinner with his family. I showed up at his house with steaks; flowers for his wife, Jen; and candy for his two boys, Tommy and Jack. After dinner, Coach Nowinsky and I sat in the backyard—him with a beer, me with iced tea—and continued to talk. Actually, looking back, it was more of me thinking out loud as I tried to piece together a timeline of my parents' problems.

I supposed they began growing apart while I was in high school. By the time I got to college, I knew something was off. I'd call my dad and tell him about a good practice or a new way I was prepping for the next week's game, and when I called home again a few days later and spoke with my mom, she wouldn't know about the previous conversation I'd had with my dad. They weren't talking to each other, I realized.

When I went home on the weekends, I noticed they didn't do things together. Dad stayed in his office, and my mom did her work upstairs or outside.

As I recounted this to Coach Nowinsky, I cringed at my naivete. Several times, without explaining my concerns, I had invited one of them to dinner near school and then at the last minute told them I'd forgotten that I'd already invited the other one. As a result, we'd all be together. My parents made the best of it. I think they understood what I was trying to do. It was always awkward.

I also went through a brief stretch at that time when I would show up at home without calling. I don't know why; maybe I hoped to walk through the door and find things back to normal, the way I remembered my childhood. Or maybe I wanted to find one or both of them up to something that would force them to share more of the story behind their split. Whatever it was, my mom wanted it stopped. "You have to tell us before you come home," she said.

"It's going to be okay," Coach Nowinsky said. "Give it time."

Coach kept a close eye on me all season. At practices, he always asked how things were going. I appreciated the way he looked out for me as a person, not just a player, and recognized that I was still a kid who wasn't really as big and strong as I looked. As the song says, "We all need someone to lean on."

Sometimes in my conversations with Coach Nowinsky, I went overboard, and even he, always so patient and understanding, had to call me on my shit. I remember one day I got on a holier-than-thou soap box, declaring that I was different from my parents and I was going to get engaged and married only once, and it was going to be forever, because I understood what it meant to honor a commitment.

Coach put his hand over his eyes and shook his head.

"You got a girlfriend, Colt?"

"No."

"Well, dude, before you talk about getting engaged and married—forever, of course—you have to at least go on a date."

That was a separate issue. Among my coaches, teammates, and three roommates, I was famously antisocial. My roommates—Mike Zimmer, Jordan Newkirk, and Corey Shandrick—were great guys who always invited me to go out with them to bars and parties, and when I said, "No, thanks," they shrugged and said, "Suit yourself." I stayed in my room, watched *Friends* on Netflix, and played video games, mostly *Call of Duty* and *Madden*.

After the football season, I spent nearly every weekend at home in Washington, staying with my grandparents after my mom and dad moved to Denver. Occasionally my roommates pressed me to stay and share in their fun. I always made up an excuse why I couldn't, usually that I was going home to see a girl. It was easier to lie instead of explaining why I didn't want to go to parties or chase girls. Then one day Mike called me out.

"Dude, there's no girl at home," he said.

"How do you know?" I asked.

"Dude, I know you," he said. "I've lived with you for a couple years. There's no girl at home. It's okay if you just admit it."

"All right," I said. "There's no girl at home. I just don't like being put in an awkward situation."

"I get it," he said, and that was it, he didn't bring it up again.

The benefit of having a straight-arrow player like me on the team did not escape the coaching staff. I remember a barbecue that Coach Nowinsky hosted at his house for the defensive linemen. There, he introduced me to Shelby Harris, a six-two, 260-pound athletic marvel who transferred from Wisconsin following a disciplinary issue. Shelby, now a star in the NFL, was a free spirit off the field, and Coach Nowinsky thought I could temper his behavior if we became friends, which we did.

"Keep Shelby safe," Coach told me. "Keep his head on straight."

It might have been more than I could handle. Shelby hosted a house party one time in the same apartment building where I lived, and his preparty was so outrageous it was shut down before the real one even started. As different as we were, Shelby represented one of the things I liked best about football. It was the way guys from different cultural, financial, and ethnic backgrounds came together and became a team. Our differences were real and oftentimes challenging, but our bonds as teammates were also real, and we got each other through battles on and off the field.

My junior season was my best one yet. Despite a torn hamstring, I led the conference in quarterback sacks and received first-team all-American honors. We also defeated our rival Appalachian State in the playoffs. Pro scouts asked to meet with me. Agents called my dad and Coach Nowinsky. As time passed, a sense of normalcy returned, a new normal, and some of the wounds felt like they were also healing. I visited my parents in Denver, where my dad took me to dinner and, with tears in his eyes, told me that he wanted to date and hopefully meet someone special. He was lonely by himself, he said.

My mom had a rougher time restarting her life. But the next time I visited Denver, she was getting out and dating. I was proud of her. My dad, meanwhile, was sharing a condo with a woman he would soon marry, Leigh, and her four children, ages nine through fourteen. They were as nice and warm as I'd expect my dad would want in his life, and now they're my bonus family. I love 'em all. But back then I remember looking at my dad and thinking, *Man, you just got me and Connor out of the house on full-ride scholarships. What are you doing?*

What I came to understand then was that my parents were still my parents—and they'll always be my parents. I still loved them as we navigated this new chapter in our lives. My dad is my best friend, and my mom is my confidante whose opinion I will always get whether I want or need it, and though our family dynamic has changed, we'll continue to figure out these new territories as we always had: together.

It was all going to be okay.

I Don't Give Up

I went down, and as I did, every curse word I knew filled my head. But only one came out of my mouth. It was the big one. It echoed across the field with an explosive clarity matched by the pain in my knee.

It was the first game of the season, my senior year. I'd been voted team captain only a few weeks earlier. And only a few minutes earlier I had run out onto the field full of hopes of another winning record, going to the playoffs, and racking up more all-American-worthy stats. Now I just prayed my dream of an NFL career wasn't blown.

I limped off the field and went straight into the locker room, slapped on a knee brace, and returned to the game. On Sunday, we watched the film and saw someone roll up on my knee. It hurt to watch it again. The room filled with sympathetic groans. The next day, I went for an X-ray. It showed a torn LCL—the lateral collateral ligament in my right knee. Normal protocol for treating such an injury was three to five weeks of rest and rehab. I kept the brace on, popped some pain meds, and played every game the rest of the season.

Unfortunately, we didn't make the playoffs, but on a personal level, I had an outstanding season and was named to four first-team all-American lists. With my sights set on the pros, I signed with an agent and spent the winter getting myself in the best possible shape. I rehabbed my knee and strengthened my entire body at St. Vincent High Performance Training Facility in Indianapolis. I also dropped fifteen pounds to give me more speed and agility after several scouts said they saw me playing outside linebacker.

Former ISU teammates Nate Palmer, who'd been drafted the year before by the Green Bay Packers, and Mike Zimmer, who'd signed with Jacksonville, offered encouragement. They believed I was NFL material. I spoke with reporters and went on podcasts to make sure pro scouts and coaches were aware of me.

"What's your biggest strength?" the host of one college football podcast asked.

"I don't give up," I said.

I needed that resolve. When invitations went out for the NFL Scouting Combine in February, I was not among the 360 college players invited to participate. I was stunned. I was a two-time all-American. It didn't make any sense until my agent did some digging and learned that teams were concerned about my knee injury. I made up for it by participating in a Pro Day at Northwestern. Only ten of the league's thirty-two teams sent scouts, but those who were there saw me crush all the drills: the forty-yard dash, the broad jump, the vertical jump, and my position-specific tasks.

I ended the day still hopeful about the draft. My agent called and said he was already getting feedback from scouts. I was also buoyed by pep talks from Coach Nowinsky and my dad. There was no way I wasn't going to get drafted in one of the seven rounds, I thought.

Then came May 8–10, 2014: the NFL draft. Excited and nervous, I watched the live event on ESPN from my dad's house in Denver. I invited my mom to watch with us, and she said yes. The draft and my dream of getting to the NFL was that big of a deal.

We were all together, a new, extended, blended family, with the emphasis on family. In that respect, I already felt like a winner.

I didn't expect to get picked in the first round on day one, so I watched without feeling any anxiety, as did my family, and we had a good time, almost like old times, in front of the TV. I had a similar attitude the next day as I watched the second and third rounds. I didn't expect to hear my name, but hey, you never know for sure. Then, on day three, my agent called and told me to get ready for teams to call. He'd heard some buzz about me, he said.

According to him, the drill was simple and straightforward. Teams would call and have a quick chat to see where my head was at, to see if I was also interested in them. As I told my agent, I was interested in any NFL team that wanted me. But the third round came and went without a call. As did the fourth, fifth, and sixth rounds. I was terribly depressed and feeling like my dream had failed to materialize despite working my ass off for my whole life when the seventh round started and the phone rang.

It was Jim Harbaugh, the head coach of the San Francisco 49ers. His team had three picks in the seventh round and from the things he said and the way he kept me on the line throughout the round, without letting me hang up, I figured I had to be one of them. As we chatted, I missed calls from the Bills, the Chargers, the Colts, and the Raiders.

My dad wrote down the numbers and relayed them to my agent. It was a genuine cluster of me talking to Coach Harbaugh, missed calls, my dad on his cell phone with my agent, background chatter, and anticipation. Everyone was poised to hear my name and celebrate. The room felt like it might burst at any second.

Then I saw my buddy Shelby Harris get drafted by the Oakland Raiders.

"For real?" I said.

Shelby hadn't played a single down the entire year after getting booted for conduct issues.

"How the hell did he get drafted and not you?" my dad said.

Then, very quickly, it was over. Despite all the time I spent on the phone with Coach Harbaugh, the 49ers didn't draft me. He ended the call abruptly, and I looked around the room in a daze. None of the other teams had drafted me, either. I sat down on the sofa and buried my head in my hands. All that hope and anticipation evaporated. How'd that happen?

If ever I needed to be surrounded by family, it was then. I needed every single one of the hugs and words of encouragement I got that night.

Then my phone rang. I looked down and saw it was my agent.

"It's not over, man," he said. "Don't give up."

"I'm not giving up," I said.

"I'm going to make calls," he said. "Trust me, it's not over."

He was right. Though I went undrafted, over the next week, six or seven teams extended contracts to me, including the 49ers. They offered me $15,000 to sign with them, a far cry from the $14.5 million bonus given to that year's number one pick, Jadeveon Clowney. Still a little salty toward them for keeping me on the phone without drafting me, I said no, thanks. As for the other teams, my agent and I went over the list and considered which of them were most in need of a linebacker. I signed with the San Diego Chargers.

The Chargers' rookie camp started in mid-May, two days after Mother's Day. Eager and motivated, I gave it my all during the three-day workout. The coaches praised my performance in the seven-on-seven and nine-on-seven drills alongside the team's top picks, Jason Verrett and Jeremiah Attaochu, who became a good friend. I returned for mini-camp in June, and two months later, I was at regular training camp with the veterans.

This was the dream: I was suited up and on the field with the team's future Hall of Fame quarterback Philip Rivers, all-pro free safety Eric Weddle, and one of my childhood idols, linebacker Dwight Freeney, who had signed with the team the year before and was himself on the mend from a season-ending injury the previous September. One afternoon, as I walked back to my hotel from the practice facility, Freeney pulled up next to me in his Range Rover and offered me a ride. I got in with my hero and played it cool until I was back in my hotel room. Then I called my dad and turned into a ten-year-old again.

"Guess what?" I said. "You're never going to believe it. I got a ride from Freeney. Dwight freakin' Freeney, dude. He just dropped me off at my hotel."

In my first preseason game, I made two tackles, including a fifteen-yard sack of the opposing quarterback. I also generated a respectable number of laughs the night the rookies put on a show for the veterans. I did an impression of veteran linebacker Tom Keiser and a shameless rendition of some nineties hit song I can't remember (probably for the best). I felt like the coaching staff saw me as a guy who added value to the team. My dad even flew into town to watch me play and soak up some of the NFL atmosphere.

He was still there when I suffered a crisis. The team had ordered me a new supply of contact lenses, solution, and cleaner. When delivery was delayed, they provided substitutes. But what I thought was a new bottle of solution turned out to be cleaner. I soaked my contacts in it overnight and popped them in my eyes the next morning before going to practice. By the time I got to the facility, my eyes were red and burning. I thought it was bad allergies.

But the burning intensified. Between plays, I ran to the side and put ice cubes on my eyes. Then cold rags and ice. Then I couldn't take the pain anymore. I was pulled from practice, put in a dark room, and given Vicodin, which I had a reaction to. It made me extremely anxious about everything, to the point where I lost control and screamed for a doctor.

The team's head trainer rushed me to the ER, where I was given morphine and examined by an ophthalmologist. His diagnosis sounded like something from a horror movie. The contacts I'd soaked in cleanser had etched themselves into my eyeballs. I had circular burns almost down to my cornea.

"I don't know how the hell you practiced," he said. "You were literally burning holes in your eyes as you played."

Luckily for me, eyes heal quickly, and I needed only a couple weeks before I was ready to play. Several players advised me to sue the team and the league. I knew no team would ever touch me again if I filed a lawsuit. My options were limited. Try to win a few million dollars in the courtroom at the cost of my future in the NFL or work my ass off on the field to make the team. After talking it through with my dad, I put on a pair of purple rec specs and kept playing.

At the end of camp, in late August, the team finalized its roster for the start of the regular season, and my name wasn't on it. If effort and toughness were all that was required, I would've made the team easily. As I was well aware, though, many other factors came into play when the coaching staff made their final cuts, and so when the Chargers' general manager Tom Telesco called me into his office and turned me loose, I could tell it wasn't an easy decision.

"We don't have room for you now," he said. "We're going to put you on waivers. But you're a good kid. We like you. We'd like to keep you around."

I asked what that meant.

"You never know in this business," he said.

I nodded with what I hoped was a look of strength and understanding, while inside I asked myself a question that would later be all too familiar: How do you not know?

My two best friends from the team, Jerry Attaochu and Manti Te'o, called to wish me well before I left camp. Then I went back to Washington and moved into my grandparents' basement. I'd shipped all my stuff there after leaving college. I felt weird and rootless, disappointed and more than a little cheated.

I'd shown that I could compete in the NFL under both the best and most trying of circumstances and also, in a more intangible way, that the Chargers could count on me being a team player off the field. Despite everything I knew about the game, I still wondered how that wasn't enough. How could I want something so badly and do everything possible to get it and still not have them want me?

What's Your Number?

F ive days later, the Philadelphia Eagles called. I worked out with the team, and they signed me. I was with the team a week before getting cut again. I was told they planned to re-sign me, when there was room on the roster, perhaps in a week or two.

I returned to my grandparents' basement, expecting to return to Philly, when the Chargers signed me to their practice squad. Despite a bag full of dirty clothes next to my bed, I got on a plane the next day and flew to San Diego. The Chargers welcomed me back and made me feel like a part of the team.

As a member of the practice squad, I played every day except Sundays. My job was to help the guys on the team get ready for that week's game. We practiced Tuesday, Wednesday, and half of Thursday, and had a walk-through on Friday. I took the role seriously, pushing myself as hard as any starter on the team. Every morning I was in the weight room by 4:30 a.m. Then I hit the sauna, steam room, and hot tub, so my body was warm and ready for whatever the coaches planned for the day.

One day I arrived to find a package had been placed in my locker. A practice guy receiving any kind of mail was unheard of, never mind a package; only star players received such deliveries. Several guys watched as I opened the box and pulled out my practice jersey from the Eagles. There was also a handwritten note from Eagles' head coach Chip Kelly, thanking me for a hard week of practice and play.

The guys gave me a fist bump.

"Classy."

"Way to bring it."

"Only way."

As the season got underway, I responded to the routine of life as a pro football player. After practice, I packed up dinner from the spread of food put out at the facility and went back to the Holiday Inn, where I had a spacious corner room. I ate and went to bed by 8:30 or 9:00 p.m. I hung out with Jerry Attaochu and Manti Te'o and enjoyed getting to know about them and their lives. Jerry had lived in Nigeria until he was eight, then moved to Washington, DC, and gone to college at Georgia Tech. Manti, who intercepted a Tom Brady pass in the fourth game of the season, came from a Polynesian family.

Exposure to such diversity was one of my favorite aspects of being in the NFL. I was open to broadening my life and view of the world. I started going to a local church and gradually reaffirming my faith in God—and faith in myself. It was very much due to looking around and being grateful for the position I was in.

I continued to feel that way when I was invited back to training camp at the start of the next season. Knowing a job wasn't guaranteed, I made sure my play stood out on the practice field, but in this world where actions spoke louder than words, it was actually something I said that made the biggest impression. One afternoon, after a film-study session, our linebacker coach suggested we play a team bonding game and take turns getting up in front of the room and making fools of ourselves.

Each player had the choice of whether to tell a joke or field the question—any question whatsoever, no subjects off-limits. This was pro sports, and everybody understood that whatever was said in that room stayed in the room. When my turn came, I didn't have a joke, so I walked to the front of the room and said, "Hit me with a question."

"What's your number?"

The question came so fast I wasn't even sure who asked it.

"What do you mean?" I asked.

"How many girls have you slept with?" someone clarified.

"Yeah, what's your number, baby?" someone else chimed in.

I immediately thought, *Oh shit.*

I knew what they were probably thinking: double digits. To most of them, I was a pretty boy who had an easy time with the ladies. I did nothing to dispel such impressions, in fact, and even contributed to them with white lies and noncommittal nods and assertions when stories were told in the locker room. Basically, I went along with shit, the same as I had in college. But for reasons I still don't understand, after years of avoiding any such admission, I couldn't avoid it that day. Actually, I didn't want to avoid it. I simply felt compelled to share the truth, and with a here-goes-nothing gulp of air, I said, "Zero."

It was met with silence.

No one expected to hear that number, including me. The room was stunned into momentary silence.

"Say what, playboy?" someone finally said.

"Zero."

I thought my admission would be met with teasing and laughter, and indeed, I heard someone exclaim, "Oh shit," and another guy said, "Underwood, man, I know someone who can help fix that." But I think what surprised those guys more than anything else was my honesty. They were 100 percent supportive. "Pretty cool," one guy said. Another added, "Damn, I wish I was, too." There was the expected wisecrack, too. But I laughed harder than anyone when someone quipped, "I still don't get it. How'd you get this far looking the way you look and not get your ding-dong done?"

Good question.

My sex life—or lack of one—was one of those things that, over time, became *one of those things*. I was a high school freshman when a junior named Bari Marder became the recipient of my first kiss. Two years later, I dated Rachel Filler, a freshman, for about four or five months. I was too focused on football to have any other extracurriculars, like a girlfriend or a social life. Between workouts, practices, and games, I had very little spare time.

During my senior year, I dated Deanne Holmes, who was a senior and a popular student and cheerleader. I was the captain of the football team. We were a match made in high-school-couples heaven. After every high school game, we went to the Steak 'n Shake and hung out with classmates. Deanne was queen of the party. I often felt I was pretending to be someone other than myself. High school is like that, I suppose.

The whole social thing came naturally to Deanne. She also liked to party, and I'd yet to take my first sip of beer. She could talk and laugh all night, and I pretty much stayed wrapped up inside myself. The more time we spent together, the more I realized we were opposites. This was especially true when we got to making out. We were genuinely attracted to each other, but she was interested and willing to go faster and further than me.

We'd get to a point where I was uncomfortable and say I had to go home. I'd make up some excuse like I forgot to let the dog out or I promised to help my mom. My inability to explain myself made it extremely awkward.

Then there was a party at her house one night, and several of us—two other couples and a random person—were sitting on a large, semicircular sectional couch, watching a movie. Deanne and I were together under a blanket. I sensed that she wanted to do more than I was ready for. Speaking softly, I explained that I was uncomfortable with other people nearby.

How did I not know?

I just didn't.

When I saw Deanne the next day, I sensed some weirdness between us and walked away without saying anything. Later that day, I broke up with her.

I'm still sorry about the way that went down. I wish I'd possessed the maturity to discuss what had happened and why I'd called a time-out. I might've been able to explain that I had felt scared and unsure of myself, something few would have dared suspect of someone my size and stature, and as captain of the football team, including Deanne.

People make assumptions all the time based on what seems obvious, and what we learn over and over again is that the obvious isn't always so.

After Deanne and I broke up, rumors flew around school that I was gay. I assumed the reason why. The rumor became so rampant in our small town, even my mom heard about it. We were in the car one day, at a red light, when out of nowhere she said, "You know, Colt, we'd still love you and support you if you were gay."

Embarrassed, I let her know that I'd heard the rumors, too, but they were just that, rumors. I was straight. It wasn't my first time addressing that subject. When I was in ninth grade, I ordered porn on TV, straight and gay. My dad saw a $90 charge on the cable bill and told me he'd kick my ass if I did that again. He was right, of course; porn was free on the Internet. Unfortunately, that got me in trouble, too. One day the following year I was playing basketball in the backyard when my dad called me into his office and motioned toward his computer screen.

"Do you want to explain this?" he said.

He'd called up the history of recent Google searches, which included gay porn sites and a variety of questions: *Am I gay? How do you know if you're gay? Why don't I like having sex with my girlfriend?* At first, I denied responsibility. Then I owned up to having been curious. He asked if I wanted to talk about it. I said no, explaining that I'd figured things out on my own.

I begged him not to tell Mom. I'm sure he did. But neither of them ever spoke about it with me.

All that research, though, led me to understand that I was definitely attracted to girls. But as with all immersion therapy, even my own self-styled Internet version, it didn't change who I was or cure me of my fears. It was then, as a way of protecting myself from all the stuff about relationships that gave me anxiety, I decided I would stay a virgin until I fell in love with someone. That became my safe zone.

Sometimes I wonder if my life would have been much easier if I had been gay. Maybe it would've helped me to know myself better and sooner. Maybe I wouldn't have stayed a virgin. Maybe I wouldn't have asked *Who am I?* as often as I did and suffered as much angst because I didn't have an answer. Identity was such a big question mark with me. Yes, I was a football player. But what else was I? Was there anything more?

At seventeen, I wanted answers and didn't understand that not knowing and, in fact, having to figure out my own answers through trial and error (lots of error) was part of the process. I didn't realize people keep asking those questions throughout their lives. As I later found out, my own parents were asking themselves those questions.

Of course, none of that history was apparent when I stood in front of my Charger teammates and admitted my most intimate secret, that I was, at twenty-three years old, still a virgin. No one asked for an explanation, whether my reasons were religious or otherwise. No one asked if I was gay. It didn't matter to them. We were teammates, brothers on and off the field, and they were supportive of me, as I was of them. As far as they were concerned, my number, whatever it happened to be, was fine as long as I was comfortable with it.

There was, in fact, no magic number, and no reason to be embarrassed that mine was zero. I owned it.

But ownership and hope it might one day change were two different things. I thought about what it would be like to fall in love. I saw myself with a family of my own. I just didn't know when any of that would happen or how I would know I was ready. Football was still my everything. There wasn't much room for anything else. I didn't do much of anything else. But, as one of my teammates liked to say, you gotta have faith, baby. So I told myself to stay open, look for signs, maybe even look for a date, and keep the faith.

Done

In one of the final preseason practices, I pulled my hamstring, and unfortunately, that was it for me and the Chargers. The team waived me injured and gave me credit for the season. It was a bittersweet parting. My leg needed eight weeks to heal properly. I rehabbed at St. Vincent in Indianapolis, and then worked out with the Green Bay Packers, Cleveland Browns, Indianapolis Colts, and Oakland Raiders. The Raiders liked what they saw and signed me to their practice squad in December 2015. I was relieved to have a job.

I moved to Oakland and immersed myself in the new system. Putting on the iconic black-and-silver uniform made me feel like a kid in costume, except the fun and excitement I should've felt wasn't there. It was my third uniform in two years, and it underscored the fact that this was a business, not a game. I was in the NFL, but, as I was experiencing, it was more grind than glory, and it was grinding me down, physically, emotionally, and spiritually.

Sensing this perhaps, Raiders quarterback Derek Carr invited me to the team's Bible study. If I'd been in a better place, I probably would've sloughed it off. But I took the invitation as a sign that I ought to give it a try. What did I have to lose?

The Bible study met every Thursday morning. I listened as Derek and several of the guys with deeper understanding of the Bible dissected verses and stories that had been thoughtfully selected for the team. A lively discussion always followed. More than anything, though, these meetings were great bonding experiences. Guys opened up and confided things I would've never expected or admitted, including their own uncertainties about life.

I was impressed by their honesty and inspired by the role faith played in their lives. I was trying to figure out the same thing. What role did faith play in my life? I only called on God when I needed him. That wasn't the way it worked. Realizing any relationship I developed with God had to be on a more regular basis, I started to read Bible passages every night and made time every day to reflect and meditate on where my life was at.

One place it wasn't: happy. I still talked on a regular basis with Coach Nowinsky, and one day I was on the phone with him when the truth just came out of my mouth with a clarity that surprised even me.

"Man, I miss college ball," I said. "I had way more fun there than the pros."

Aware that I needed to do something more meaningful with my life, I waited until the season ended in January and then launched the Colton Underwood Legacy Foundation, a nonprofit to provide equipment and resources to people living with cystic fibrosis. I was inspired by my four-year-old cousin Harper, one of thirty thousand people in the United States born with the genetic disorder. She was a pint-size warrior who took fourteen pills a day to stay alive. Through her mom, my aunt Shannon, I learned about the life-threatening struggles of other children who didn't come from Harper's same fortunate financial situation, and I decided to help.

I organized a football camp in Washington for 450 kids and almost by accident raised $50,000. Afterward, I went to the local CF clinic in Peoria and asked, "What do you need?" We purchased aerodynamic bicycles for cardio testing and two brand-new breathing machines. It was one of the most fulfilling days of my life.

It was like I'd found a new piece to the puzzle that was me. I liked helping other people, and I was going to keep doing it.

I decided to keep playing football, too. At the end of May I arrived in Napa Valley at the first Raiders OTA (organized team activity) of the season. For players at my level, this was a kind of pre-preseason. Aware this was my make-or-break year in terms of moving up from the practice squad to the full-time-players roster, I invested nearly $15,000 of my own money in a personal trainer and got in as good shape as any linebacker in the league.

As the OTA opened, I attended the initial meeting for the entire defense. When I loaded my iPad with the new playbook, instead of finding the schematics for defense, I saw the playbook for the offense. I thought it was an error until the line coach tapped me on the shoulder, pulled me out of the meeting, and informed me that I had been recategorized as a tight end. No one had told me that I'd been moved to offense.

I sat through a very different type of meeting with the offense. Beyond the fact that there were hundreds of new, complex plays to learn, I was clueless as to why the coaches switched my position without even mentioning it to me. I hadn't played offense since high school. Even then, I'd played fullback, not tight end. I couldn't remember the last time I ran a route or caught a pass. It didn't make any sense.

Although I offered up a can-do, whatever's-best-for-the-team attitude, privately my head was a mess. Then one day I noticed a card on the bulletin board outside the locker room offering confidential help with mental health. After practice and from the privacy of my hotel room, I called the number and made an appointment. Early in our first session, she asked why I hadn't seen a therapist before and, for whatever reason, that one simple question opened a floodgate of not-so-simple personal revelations.

I told her everything—everything I thought was contributing to the stress, pressure, and anxiety I felt in regard to football and family and how the two overlapped.

"Do you enjoy what you do?" she asked.

"Not really," I said.

"Then why are you doing it?"

"It's my job."

"And?"

"I don't want to let anyone down, especially my dad," I said.

Talking helped clarify things. So did LASIK surgery in June. But then, a few days later, something happened that would change my focus and make my future come into view.

I was in the back of an Uber, telling my driver about my recent surgery, when my mom called and said my dog Bullet needed to be put down. The unexpected news hit me straight in the gut. I'd raised Bullet and my other Lab, Sniper, since they were puppies. We'd hiked and played together and cuddled at night. They heard all my secrets, bad dog jokes, and worst singing of songs—and still they loved me unconditionally.

I burst into tears, caught the next plane to Denver, and said goodbye to my dog. When I met with my therapist again, I told her that I was done with football. I was depressed—and done. I knew it as soon as I hung up with my mother, I explained. I wanted to be with my dog instead of on the practice field. I was wasting my time playing football.

"If you want to be done with football, what's next?" she asked.

"I'm going to finish out the season," I said.

"Why? Does that make sense?"

"Yes and no," I said. "I signed a contract. I'll honor that commitment. Then I'll see what happens."

What happened is that I returned to the Raiders' preseason training camp in August and on the third day of camp—our first in pads—I ran a flat route, went to catch the ball, and got blown up. Kaboom. Stars. Extreme pain. I'd been hit hard before, and delivered some nasty hits of my own, but I didn't remember feeling anything close to this kind of pain. I thought my back had been broken. Slowly, carefully, I got up. I unstrapped my helmet, threw it on the ground, and walked into the locker room. I was done—or should've been.

The training staff and team doctor met me in the locker room. They cut off my jersey while I described, to the best of my ability, what had happened, including the terrifying sound of a couple pops and cracks. They acknowledged my injury, and after a brief exam, they diagnosed it as an AC sprain—a bad twist and pull of the ligaments around the shoulder's acromioclavicular joint. They said I should be good to play again in five days.

I didn't buy their diagnosis. I'd heard pops and cracks. My entire upper body was killing me. I couldn't lift up my arm without excruciating pain. It hurt to breathe. When I asked how they knew it was only a sprain without an MRI or X-ray, the trainer called me a pussy. I called my agent, who told me to insist on an MRI. That only brought me dirty looks from those on the team who'd examined me. They wanted to know why I didn't trust their diagnosis.

After I pushed them, they scheduled an MRI. When I asked about the results, they said it matched their thoughts and I should be good to go soon. Five days later, I suited up again, taped a thigh pad on top of my shoulder pads, and ran out to the practice field. I screamed through every drill from the excruciating pain. I couldn't catch a pass or throw a block. I couldn't even lift my arm. I could barely put my socks on.

That I was even out there could be attributed to only two things: a superhuman toughness and equally incredible stupidity. Finally, at the end of August, the Raiders cut me. I was relieved. At least now my body had the time it needed to heal.

A few days later, my agent called to say he'd lined up a try-out with the Chiefs in Kansas City. Was I ready to go? I couldn't even fake it. Nor did I want to. I told him I'd gone to the gym and couldn't bench press 225 pounds, never mind 300 pounds. I couldn't play. I couldn't cut my food.

I had a new mission: to get well. I saw a specialist in Vail, who took another MRI. This time I heard a much different story. I had a grade-three tear and my coracoclavicular ligament was dangling. There was a separation of the AC joint, too, and the shoulder itself was fractured. It was much worse than I expected. I needed surgery.

I informed the Raiders of my condition, expecting them to cover the costs. Team officials pretty much said it wasn't their responsibility. I disagreed and filed an injury grievance with the NFL. My career was over.

On a brighter note, I sensed my life might be starting in a whole new and exciting direction. Not that I had anything specific in mind. But when those close to me asked what was next for me, I said something that caught everyone off guard.

"I'm going on a date."

Falling in Love

It's impossible to remember all the times that people have tried to set me up on a date. From high school through college and the pros, I was always the guy without a girlfriend, always the guy who was free on the weekend, always the guy with nothing planned, always the guy who was single, always the guy about whom they said, "You gotta meet him. He's a pro football player. He's six foot three. He's got short blond hair, blue eyes, and yeah, he's cute." And then they added, "No, he's not gay. Unbelievable, right?"

This is what I was told:

"You'll love her. She's great."

"You'll be perfect together. She's great."

"She's your type—athletic, smart, funny, good values, very chill. She's great."

"I showed her your Facebook page. She thinks you're hot."

"She saw your Instagram. She thinks you're hot."

"She thinks you're hot and can't believe you aren't taken or gay."

I always managed to conjure up an excuse as to why I wasn't available, even though each girl sounded perfect, like the person I'd been saving myself for, the girl who was going to challenge and motivate me, make me laugh, be able to chill, and also be driven to achieve on her own. I always joked that I didn't want finding love to be easy, and it wasn't. I did everything possible to ensure I was never going to find it, even though when I said I wanted to date, marry, and have a family of my own, I was telling the truth.

You didn't have to be a therapist to diagnose what was going on. It was called *avoidance*. With a capital *A*. I did everything I could to keep myself out of situations that would be uncomfortable, stressful, or awkward, including grabbing a drink or meeting for coffee. And a movie? Forget it. I was either pathological or downright weird, I really didn't spend time analyzing the reasons. It was just easier to say no.

That is, until my Raiders teammate Andrew East suggested I ask his wife's best friend out on a date. We were getting ready to play the Packers in the third game of the preseason. Andrew was the team's long snapper. He'd been married for four months to former gymnast Shawn Johnson, who'd won four medals (one gold and three silvers) in the 2008 Olympics and captured the first-place Mirrorball Trophy on ABC's *Dancing with the Stars*. She was at the Summer Olympics in Rio, doing commentary for Yahoo! Sports.

Andrew and I had gotten together to watch the US women's gymnastics on TV, marveling as they executed their routines with grace, power, and precision. He shared a lot of insider info about them—Simone Biles, Gabby Douglas, Madison Kocian, Laurie Hernandez, and Aly Raisman. After the team captured a gold medal, he asked what I thought about Aly, a dark-haired beauty from Massachusetts. He said Shawn was always trying to find her a boyfriend.

"Do you want to send Aly a video congratulating her and maybe see if she wants to grab drinks when she's out here?"

She had a gymnastics tour lined up after the Olympics, he said, and San Jose was on the schedule.

"Does she even know who I am?" I asked.

"Yeah, we've already told her about you," he said. "Come on. Just do it, and Shawn will give it to her."

"Sure, why not?" I said.

I went out on the practice field and taped a video congratulating Aly and asking her to let me know if she wanted to go on a double date with me and Andrew and Shawn when she was next in San Jose. I thought Shawn would give the video directly to her. Instead it was shown to Aly while she was being interviewed (not by Shawn) and livestreamed on Yahoo! The setup was cute, I have to admit. She was asked about the kind of guy she'd like to date: After she ruled out Zac Efron (he belonged to Simone) and New England Patriots superstar Rob Gronkowski (too big of a partier), she was handed a cell phone and told there was a message on it from some guy.

"Did Shawn put you up to this?" she asked, smiling nervously.

Then she played my video. I felt bad for Aly being put on the spot, and I was embarrassed when the video of her watching my video and my video on its own both went viral. It would've been even more embarrassing if she'd said no. But she didn't. She gamely said she'd go on a date with me, and I found myself feeling incredibly relieved and, strangely, even more excited.

Andrew gave me her number, and I texted her a private and more personal hello and congratulations. Aly replied, and soon we were involved in a protracted back-and-forth. She had no time to waste and said we shouldn't even start talking if it didn't seem like we weren't going to be able to meet in person. She preferred actual conversations over texts, she explained. I was the same way. I let her know that I was staying at my dad's house in Denver while I waited to have surgery on my shoulder. She was going to be in Denver in two days.

"Perfect," I said. "Let's go out to dinner."

Hoping to avoid another viral moment, we kept our dinner low-key. We slipped into a corner table for two at Guard and Grace, the best steakhouse in Denver, and talked for hours. I wanted to know about the Olympics, and she asked about my injury and upcoming surgery. Aly was easy to talk to. She was open, funny, bright, honest, and inquisitive. She laughed easily and had a smile that I would've been happy to simply gaze at for the rest of the night, no further conversation necessary.

It was very late when I dropped her back at her hotel, and when I said I'd had a great time, I meant it. Later that night, Aly texted me a thank-you. Neither of us had expected to get on as well as we did. For a first date, it couldn't have gone better.

But I had no idea whether there'd be a second date or when I'd even speak to her again. She was off on the Kellogg's Tour of Gymnastics Champions, a three-month showcase of the country's best men and women gymnasts, stopping in thirty-six cities across the United States. I wondered when the right time to call her would be. How soon would be too soon? As it turned out, I didn't have to worry. We spoke later that night and FaceTimed with each other every night for the next two weeks. It was like being together without being together.

At the end of September, we had our second in-person date in Dallas. We'd talked ahead of time about where I was going to stay and decided we'd share a room. I didn't say anything, but that scared me. Though we had exchanged so many personal details with each other over FaceTime, this was different. I decided to go with the flow, and that turned out to be the right choice. We had dinner, talked, and made out before falling asleep together, and though I was too nervous to sleep soundly, I thought the night had been pressure-free, relatively innocent, and just plain fun. I hoped Aly felt the same.

I'm pretty sure I wouldn't have seen her again if she'd felt otherwise. The next time we got together, Aly picked me up at the airport. Even in sweats, she looked beautiful. Her hair was pulled back, and her big, brown eyes were incredibly expressive. After a few minutes of small talk, she turned to me and asked if I was a virgin. The question came out of nowhere. I assumed it had to do with the night we'd spent together. I also assumed it was important to her, important enough that only one answer was possible, and that was the truth.

"Yeah," I said.

She nodded and let that information sink in.

It may have surprised her. Maybe not.

I do believe it relieved her in some way of concerns she might have had about my expectations. The slow lane was fine with both of us. We could take our time without any kind of pressure, certainly not from me.

The more time I spent with Aly, the more attractive I found her. She was funny, sharp, and cool about things. She was very mature for her age, no doubt from having to grow up fast. She was together. She worked hard in and out of the gym. Something was always going on with her. I found it hard to believe she'd never been in a serious relationship before, simply because she was a real catch. But hey, she was so busy.

I think she looked at me similarly. We were, in many ways due to our athletic careers, like two kids pretending to be adults.

Our biggest issue had to do with trust—trusting ourselves, trusting each other, trusting ourselves together. It helped that we were alike in so many ways. We were goal- and career-oriented athletes who understood the focus, sacrifice, hours, and discipline required to perform at an elite level. We were close to our families. Aly still lived at home, and I had moved into the basement of my dad's house in Denver. We cried watching *This Is Us* and approved of each other's taste in music. We left each other funny messages.

I also fell madly in like with Aly's best friend and Olympic teammate on the Kellogg's Tour, Simone Biles. Simone was like Aly's little sister. Their dazzling performances regularly left arenas packed with breathless people, including me. Then, backstage, they reveled in girlish energy and what seemed like carefree chatter.

In the middle of October, I flew to Chicago to see Aly in the latest stop on the Kellogg's Tour, and I found myself saying the L-word for the first time. I was driving, and Aly turned up the radio and held my hand. We had been together for only about a month, but our closeness felt good and natural. There, in the car, we were in our own little bubble. The music was good, and both of us were enjoying the vibe. Then a Ne-Yo song came on the radio. Aly leaned against my shoulder and said, "I love Ne-Yo."

I heard her say something else, and I let those amazing words and the sweet sound of her voice as she said them travel from my ears through my brain and into my heart. As they did, they painted my entire being a bright shade of awesome. Only a moment or two passed before I squeezed her hand and made sure she knew I felt the same way: "I love you, too."

Aly looked up at me with an expression of surprise and . . . I don't know, maybe fear. It was not what I expected, nor obviously was what I said something she'd expected to hear, and I realized I'd probably misheard her earlier. I thought, *Oh shit, massive miscommunication*, and we drove to our hotel without saying another word. Maybe it should've been funny. It's kind of funny to me now. It was definitely awkward. But there are far worse things in life than telling someone you love them.

One of them is discovering the object of such affection doesn't feel the same way. That happened when Aly and I got back to the hotel. After we got in our room, I attempted to clarify what I'd said in the car, and why, and I ended up saying it again: I love you. I saw tears in Aly's eyes. She looked away, upset and confused, and said, "I'm not quite there yet. I don't understand why. I don't know what's going on with me."

I wasn't bothered. Our relationship was still very new. I had to give Aly room. She was methodical, guarded, and in touch with her feelings, whereas I was a well-intentioned but inexperienced guy who fell in love fast, possibly too fast, and spoke without a filter. I had to hope I didn't scare her off. The good thing was, neither of us were going anyplace. The TV was on. We were in for the night and much longer, I hoped.

I Don't Understand

In early November, I finally had surgery on my shoulder. The procedure was more extensive than the doctor thought. He found torn ligaments, disintegrating bones, and even bone chips that had slipped into my pecs. An even bigger issue arose immediately after surgery: the cost of recovery. Since I was no longer covered by my NFL insurance, I went on my dad's insurance but still had to pay his deductible and co-pay for all the procedures. Every day at the surgery center cost at least $15,000.

Like millions of other Americans who face exorbitant hospital and health care costs, I couldn't afford it, not when the alternative was recovering at home for free. After waking up, I turned to my dad and said, "Let's go home."

We turned the sofa in my dad's living room into a hospital bed. I sent Aly a selfie of me lying semiconscious, bandaged like I had just been transported out of a war zone. Without heavy drugs, I might've felt that way, too. Aly sent a giant care package full of candy, magazines, tapes, and goodies she knew I'd like. The best medicine was our daily calls and FaceTime sessions. I showed her the PICC line that ran from a catheter in my shoulder to a fanny pack on my waist.

"It pumps pain meds into my shoulder every thirty minutes," I explained. "Very sexy, right?"

My mom stopped by to check on my bandages and make sure my arm was immobilized, which was the way it had to stay for at least a month. That didn't mean I had to sit still. Two weeks after surgery, I flew to Boston to be with Aly for the conclusion of her three-month gymnastics tour. It was her hometown, we decided it was a good opportunity for our two families to meet. I met her parents first. I offered her mom a bouquet of flowers with my one good arm while their gold-medalist daughter pulled my luggage into their house. The optics weren't good. I explained chivalry was just temporarily sidelined.

My dad and Leigh came in the next day. Aly's parents hosted a brunch. I assumed Aly's parents were Boston liberals; I knew my dad was a superconservative Midwesterner. It was a potentially explosive combination. I asked my dad to avoid talking politics no matter what. Yet within the first ten minutes, he and Aly's dad, Rick, had slipped off by themselves and I heard the dreaded words coming from another room: *Trump and Hillary.*

I zoned out of the conversation I was having with Aly and Leigh and eavesdropped on our dads, waiting for the bomb to go off. It never did. Everyone was on their best behavior. Then we went to the gymnastics show. We all shared a private box at the arena and had a great time watching Aly and her teammates. The meeting was a success.

In mid-December, Aly and I decided to go public with our relationship. It had been four months, and we were done hiding it. For our first big next step together, we walked the red carpet at the Sports Illustrated Sportsperson of the Year event at the Barclays Center in Brooklyn, New York. Aly looked gorgeous in a mid-length red dress and I wore a black suit. The next day we were the hot new couple on the Internet. My phone blew up with text messages. It was high school times a thousand.

Aly spent the holidays with me in Denver. On Christmas Eve

we lit the first candle for Hanukkah, and wore matching pajamas to bed for Christmas morning. I embraced our different religious beliefs as an opportunity to learn and grow. After New Year's, Aly accompanied me to the Children's Hospital in Peoria, where we met with young patients and I presented a $10,000 check from my Legacy Foundation to the Cystic Fibrosis Foundation and local cystic fibrosis clinic.

Aly shared my enthusiasm and understood my passion for the work. As she said, "It lets you take a step back and realize how lucky you are."

In early January, we attended the Golden Globes, one of Hollywood's most glamorous events. We walked the red carpet alongside the biggest stars from movies and TV and hung out inside with Aly's Olympic teammates. *People* magazine called us a "perfect 10 couple." I was perfectly happy in this relationship. It was satisfying and serious. But I was keeping a secret from Aly. Though I looked like I belonged in this glitzy, glamorous world, I was broke. My shoulder surgery, at a cost of $40,000 to me, took most of my savings. The rest went for plane tickets and hotels to see Aly. I even sold my car.

I loved her. I could tell her anything and everything—except that I had no money. I think she would've understood, told me I was being silly, and come up with a practical savings plan for me. She was there for me in a way that made me want to be there for her ten times over. She challenged me in new ways that helped me grow and inspired me to be a better person.

At the same time, Aly had her own secrets and struggles. As we continued to grow closer and more intimate, she opened up to me about a dark and disturbing episode in her life that had left serious psychological scars. Larry Nassar, the longtime doctor for the USA Gymnastics national team, had been charged with criminal sexual conduct after various investigations the past few months uncovered incidents wherein he routinely molested and abused his female patients dating back more than two decades. Some of the girls were as young as twelve. Tearfully, Aly told me that she had been among Nassar's victims.

I had a vague recollection of reading about Nassar the previous summer in the *Indianapolis Star*. I went online and reread it. The story was one of the first to have come out about this sick predator. From there, the story spread like a fast-growing cancer. In November, criminal charges were brought against Nassar. In December, he was charged with child pornography. Aly was disgusted, rightly so.

She opened up to me after the Globes, in what I now appreciate as a moment of anger, strength, and defiance that was precipitated by eighteen women filing a lawsuit in mid-January against Michigan State University, where Nassar had been a school doctor. I was staying with Aly and her family in Boston at the time. The phone rang constantly. Aly's mom had conversations with lawyers and other parents. I felt the tension and picked up on the ways this was impacting all of them. I also saw the value of having a strong family for support.

As I began to fill in some of the blanks on what Aly didn't tell me or couldn't tell me due to the healing she had to go through first, as well as the legalities being discussed in private, I felt much less restrained than her family. I wanted to find Nassar and rip his head off.

I made it a point to listen rather than ask too many questions. Any details would have to come from Aly whenever she was ready to share them, and she was still figuring out what and how much she was comfortable sharing with me, never mind strangers. She debated with herself whether to speak out publicly. (She didn't until later that year.) Just watching her go through that was painful. Her struggle with what had happened and the deep pain of the violation to her body and spirit and ability to trust only intensified as the case against Nassar took over the news.

I felt helpless. I wanted to do something. But I didn't possess any of the tools that would enable me to help her other than being kind, sensitive, patient, and available. All I could do was let her know that wasn't going to ever happen again as long as we were together. With me, she would always be safe.

It seemed she got the message. In early February, she was finally able to tell me that she loved me. Hearing her say those words in the midst of all that she was dealing with, it made me fall in love with her all over again. She was fierce, with a heart so big and deep. I wanted to take care of her that much more.

Two weeks later, she had plans to go to Houston for a party celebrating the annual *Sports Illustrated* swimsuit issue. She and Simone had both posed for the magazine. The editor said their pictures represented "all that is beautiful and strong and inspiring in women today." I agreed. I met her in Houston, and we spent the next four days together. We went to the event, she did press, and we enjoyed our cozy alone time in the hotel.

I thought everything between us was fine and good and always getting better. Now, after having gone back and looked at photos of the two of us from the *Sports Illustrated* swimsuit issue event, I see a troubled look in Aly's eyes that I wasn't aware of then. It's distant. Something else was going on inside her, something that was bigger and beyond me.

We still said I love you to each other at the airport before walking off in different directions to catch planes, her to Boston and me to Denver. The next day, as I was driving across town in my Jeep, Aly FaceTimed me and ended our relationship. I pulled over to the side of the road, stunned and unable to comprehend this was happening. Aly said she felt overwhelmed, confused, and in need of a break. Afterward, I sat in my car and cried.

I was numb for days. I reached out to Aly several times without getting any response to my calls or texts. I called Aly's best friend,

Simone Biles, hoping she could offer an explanation or insight. She couldn't. She was also surprised. Left without any answers or information, I didn't know what to do or where to turn. I went for long runs and replayed conversations in my head, wondering if I'd said or done anything wrong.

Had I come on too strong? Had I not given her enough space? Was our long-distance relationship too much space? Did she need more support?

I decided the reasons Aly had given me for the breakup were, in fact, those she had shared with me. She was confused and needed a break. There was also the very good chance she decided that I wasn't right for her. That was more than understandable. She was going through a journey of personal healing and getting ready to take her fight public. She had more than enough going on in her life.

As much as the split hurt me, I decided all I could do was support her unconditionally and pray she could one day heal those wounds and make sure she knew I would always treasure the time we did have together. Losing in love was painful, but I was a better and wiser man for having opened my heart to her.

PART TWO

Nice Guys Finish Fourth

Out of the Basement

I made a list of things I'd lost the past year.

1. MY DOG BULLET
2. FOOTBALL
3. MY GIRLFRIEND

Those were just the top three. I was also broke. At twenty-five years old, I was under the impression that I should have had my life figured out. I thought everyone had that kind of clear direction by my age. Mark Zuckerberg had launched Facebook at twenty. Tom Brady was twenty-four when he won his first Super Bowl. Justin Bieber was a superstar before he could drive. Then again, Dallas Mavericks owner Mark Cuban had just been tending bar at my age . . . but he'd become a billionaire. I didn't have a clue what I should do next, I didn't have a career lined up, and my breakup had left me gutted.

On the positive side, I still had Sniper, my black Lab. Sometimes I wondered if I was bumming him out, too. Dogs are able to sense these things in their human companions, and when Sniper curled up next to me in bed I saw in his eyes a look that implied he was not seeing a pretty picture.

He wasn't. I like routine and a schedule. I thrive on pursuing a goal and having a sense of purpose. But I had none of the above.

Without my foundation, wherein I'd recently launched a next-phase chapter called the Legacy Project, a partnership with the manufacturer of the AffloVest, to give away one of their portable breathing devices to a cystic fibrosis patient in each of the fifty states, I would've been utterly, totally lost and depressed.

As it was, I was a sad sack of woe-is-me living in my dad's basement. I didn't want to be this guy, or one of those guys who peaked in high school or college, and so I vowed to find a way out of this rut. I started by signing up for online courses and finishing the three classes I needed to get my degree. But the accomplishment felt hollow. I missed having a girlfriend. I missed having someone say they were proud of me for blazing through the courses and cheering me on as I plotted my next move.

I knew I had the power to change that, and one day, with my frustration growing daily, I actually looked at myself in the mirror and said, "Screw this. I'm going to date."

It was a declaration to get busy. To sign up on dating apps. To go to bars. To ask friends if they could set me up. There were steps to take if I wanted to date. Except I didn't do any of them. I wussed out on every opportunity I had to create a social life and instead found myself in the same hermit-like situation I'd created for myself in high school and college. Watching TV reruns on Netflix. Checking out other people on Instagram. Making stupid excuses for why I didn't have my shit together.

I knew better and got mad at myself. One afternoon I went for a walk along the 16th Street Mall, a tourist-heavy promenade lined with stores and restaurants, cafés, and brewpubs. It was the perfect antidote for what ailed me. It was outdoors, vibrating with energy, and full of people looking to have a good time.

I started walking from one of the bridges on the north end toward Commons Park on the other side. I saw a crowd in front of the Hard Rock Cafe and stopped to investigate. The crowd was actually a long line that was composed entirely of young, good-looking women. Without exaggeration, it seemed as if every attractive, single twentysomething woman in Denver was standing right in front of me. I knew God was all-knowing and all-powerful. I also knew he worked in mysterious ways. If this was his way of answering my prayers, I was ... well ... surprised that he'd heard me, impressed, and very, very grateful.

I nosed my way up the line, smiling at several girls as I looked for information. Then, bingo! There was a sign next to the door leading inside the Hard Rock:

THE BACHELOR
OPEN CASTING CALL

Ah.

I recalled watching a recent episode of *The Bachelorette* that had advertised an upcoming casting call in Denver. This was it. The show was casting for Arie Luyendyk Jr.'s season of *The Bachelor*. That explained why only women were in line. After looking around for a moment, I got ready to leave and continue my walk when a guy from the show's casting department stepped outside and looked directly at me.

"Hey, you!"

"Yeah?" I said.

"Did you come by to talk?" he asked.

"Not really," I said. "I was just walking by and—"

Moments later I was inside and following him upstairs. He'd ushered me past the line and what was apparently the first round of screening, and then put me in a room, where he sat me in front of a small digital video camera, got me a bottle of water, and began asking me questions. I played along.

"Have you heard of *The Bachelorette* or *The Bachelor* TV series?"

"Yeah, sure."

"Do you watch them?"

"Not regularly."

"Why are you here?"

"I was just out for a walk."

"Would you consider going on *The Bachelorette*?"

"I guess. Yeah, probably."

"Tell me what's going on with you?"

"Nothing."

"But?"

"I just broke up with my girlfriend and I'm in a kind of funk. I don't feel like right now I'm in a position to really put myself out there, and it's not like I've thought about it—you know, I was just walking past . . . but now that you got me thinking, it could be a cool way to meet a nice, interesting woman."

"Have you ever been in love?"

"Yes," I said.

I wanted to be honest but without volunteering too much about myself. I certainly didn't want to mention I'd just broken up with an Olympic gold-medal gymnast. I was also nervous about what Aly might think if word about this interview ever got out. Not that we had spoken, but I still had feelings for her, and all of a sudden I began to remember what that felt like, to have those kind of feelings for someone.

"When I'm in love, I'm all in and looking for it to be reciprocated," I said. "I don't know. This could be good for me. It would force me to date. I wouldn't be able to backpedal myself out of the situation, as I tend to do. I'm a good guy, I think. But I may have a tendency to self-sabotage. I get scared. I can think of ten thousand reasons why something might not work, and I wouldn't be able to do that on the show."

I heard myself blabbering and I shut up. That was enough.

"All right, that was good," he said, setting a manila envelope in front of me. "Take that packet. Fill out the paperwork inside. Then send it back. And make a self-video when you get home."

"What do you want me to say in the video?" I asked.

"There is a list of questions inside the packet," he said. "Run through the questions. It's like interviewing yourself."

"And then?"

"It all gets reviewed," he said. "You never know. Maybe you'll get on the show."

I laughed. "Yeah, right."

I went downstairs and filled out a form with my contact information. A young woman sat down across from me with a questionnaire of her own, longer and more in-depth than mine. As both of us wrote, she asked how much information I was putting in my answers. She pouted and said "Not fair" when I explained that mine asked only for my phone number and email since I'd already chatted on video. She asked if I could help with some of her answers. "Whatcha got?" I asked.

She looked down at the paper and read, " 'Describe the type of man you're looking for.' " I waited for her to share more information, like the part she was having trouble with. "And?" I said. She smiled. "Can I just put you?"

Oh my God, was this what I was in for? I had no idea how to flirt the way she just did with me. I wondered if I was ready for this next step and any that might follow. There was only one way to find out. When I got back to my dad's house, I opened the packet, pulled out the questionnaire, and filled in the blanks

Essentially, it was a mini biography. I said that I was a professional athlete and philanthropist, with a bachelor's degree, and quickly scribbled "No" in the spaces that asked whether I'd been arrested, convicted of a crime, engaged, or married. I wondered why they grouped questions about criminal background and relationship status together. It never dawned on me that someone might see a connection.

Another block of questions asked about past relationships and whether I was genuinely interested in getting married. I said that I'd been in only one serious relationship previously, for six months, explaining that it ended because we were in different places in our careers. I definitely wanted to find someone to share my life, I wrote, adding that I was quite serious about it, too. I had a great life, I wrote, and felt it was time to take that next step.

Listing pets and hobbies was easy—black Lab, hiking, camping, working out—and the only thing that saved me from sounding like a stereotypical bro/jock from Colorado was the addition of my favorite drink: sangria. Not many guys in Denver coming off a day on the trails asked for a glass of sangria with an extra slice of orange.

I liked the challenge of describing myself in three words. I wrote: "Creative, compassionate, and charming." I think that's still accurate. There was one question that cut right to the heart of the matter and caused me to laugh when I saw it because it was so obvious and unique to this situation: Why did I want to find my future wife on a TV show?

It was a great question—and just so incredibly weird. Who went on TV to find a potential wife? I did. And the reason I gave? "I don't put myself out there enough in the real world." Translation: "I need help!"

The next day I made my video, popped the questionnaire in the mail, and completely forgot about it.

Congratulations

For the next four months, I was consumed by medical reports, legal papers, and negotiations leading to a settlement of my grievance against the Oakland Raiders. The process was like arguing on the playground in third grade, with each side basically calling the other a liar, except those involved were adults and I had a pile of X-rays and some big-ass scars as evidence. I wouldn't wish this kind of tedium on my worst enemy. It was life in hell, and every day I prayed for relief.

Then, out of the blue, my prayers were answered in the form of a letter informing me that I'd made it through to the next round of casting for *The Bachelorette*. I'd forgotten about the video and questionnaire I'd sent in. But all of a sudden it all came back to me: the Hard Rock, the women, the dude from casting who'd said, "You never know." I dropped a couple of WTF bombs and read the letter again before it really registered with me.

They were inviting me to continue the casting process on one of three upcoming dates in Los Angeles. I turned to Sniper, who was lying on the kitchen floor, and said, "Do you hear that—I'm going to LA." My dog didn't get up, but I think he wagged his tail. My dad, Leigh, and all the others offered a much better reaction, some high fives and encouragement. In this next stage, I explained to them, the producers would get to know me better as they looked to cast season fourteen of *The Bachelorette.*

I arrived at the show's Burbank production office at the end of October. There was a reception area, and the walls were decorated with framed posters from different seasons of *The Bachelor* and *The Bachelorette.* Beyond the entry, I saw a bunch of offices and cubicles. It was a busy place. Lots of people, lots of work in progress. It felt busy and chaotic, but like the people working there were having fun.

I went into a conference room and met six people from production and casting. They ranged in age from a few years older than me to their midthirties or early forties and wore hip, casual-style clothes that made them seem like they were dressed for a Saturday even though it was the middle of the week. They asked questions based on the answers I'd already submitted. I added that I'd combined this trip to LA with some post-career training provided by the NFL. I was trying to figure out what was next, I said.

I also added that I was trying to lose some weight, which elicited a few eye rolls across the table. I explained that I gained weight quickly and wasn't working out as intensely as I would've liked since my shoulder was still tender, and blah blah blah.

They seemed amused by my little obsession with my weight. It was probably unexpected. Before I left, one of the people in the room mentioned they were posting pictures online the following day of all the girls on the upcoming season of *The Bachelor.* She suggested I look at their photos, read their bios, and let them know which girls I liked.

I understood this was about more than just letting them know who I liked. They wanted to assess whether my taste aligned with theirs. In that moment, I realized the inherent tension that made the show work: the people participating on camera were looking for love, and those behind the camera were looking to make great television. Football had honed my instincts to look for the strategy. Everyone had an agenda, including me.

On the flight back to Denver, I realized I was officially obsessed with getting on *The Bachelorette*. I was thinking about it nonstop, like I had OCD. I wasn't like that a few days earlier; my attitude was more *let me see what's up*. After going to their office and talking to all those people, though, I emerged a convert. And hopefully a contender. I wanted them to pick me. Memories of my football career. I wanted to make the team. But my reasons were in line with the show's purpose: I wanted to fall in love and get engaged.

I laughed at myself as I realized how crazy that made my life seem, not to mention how crazy it sounded: finding love on a reality TV show. Was it possible? Absolutely. *The Bachelorette* was going into season fourteen and, as I knew from my recent meetings, the show boasted its share of success stories, including original couple Trista Rehn and Ryan Sutter and more recently JoJo Fletcher and Jordan Rodgers, a former football player like me.

To me, the shows were similar to dating apps—just more public. They put thirty possibilities in front of one lucky person. They created opportunities that were left more to chance in normal, everyday life. The producers were matchmakers/psychologists/cool friends working to find people who might like each other and create introductions. It all made perfect sense, even though, as I said, I knew it was downright silly to think it might work for me.

At the same time, it might. My whole life up to this point was strange. I'd played in the NFL. I'd dated an Olympic gold medalist. I'd walked the red carpet at the Golden Globes. I'd been in *People* magazine. I was a twenty-five-year-old virgin. So . . . why not *The Bachelorette*? Why wouldn't I go on TV to meet a woman and perhaps fall in love and get engaged?

I stared out the window of the plane. I realized that my head was literally in the clouds. Thoughts raced through my mind. How awesome would it be if this actually happened? If I met someone cool? If we fell in love? And got engaged?

Then came the bumps—turbulence as the plane approached the Rockies. It was a reminder to slow down. First I had to get on the show.

How many other guys had also gone in for a similar meet-and-greet interview? I had no idea. Maybe fifty, possibly one hundred or more.

I had work to do.

Once I got back home, I fired up my laptop, got on the Internet, and immersed myself in all things *Bachelorette*. I watched past seasons and read recaps. I dived into comments and familiarized myself with the fan base. I visited Bachelor Nation and liked what I saw. I found the same level of fanaticism, insider's knowledge, and passion as the NFL. Like football fans, those in Bachelor Nation were deeply involved in and opinionated about everything that happened on- and off-screen. They were already posting thoughts about the newly posted roster of girls participating on the new season of *The Bachelor*.

I went and found this list and went through it carefully, as the producers had instructed. I studied every picture and read every bio. I was mindful of my first impressions. I noted my immediate favorites and then I went back and looked again, keeping in mind all the things that caught my attention—physical attraction, interests, career, a smile, a look in her eye, and so on. Then I looked for that something extra. As in sports, there was always something else, some intangible quality that made someone stand out.

And that's what the producers wanted, right? They'd asked me to send them my top three choices. I realized it was another part of the screening process, a way for them to get a sense of the type of women I found attractive.

From research on the Internet, I knew the current season had already started to shoot; I had seen spoilers and speculation online. Fans were already debating who would be among Arie's final three. Although it was months before the season even premiered, those super sleuths somehow had a pipeline inside the show and their three favorites were Becca Kufrin, Lauren Burnham, and Tia Booth. They were my favorites, too. I sent their names to the show's producers. I also followed them on Instagram.

Per the show's rules, their accounts were set to private. They had to accept my request to follow them before I could see any photographs on their page. None of them did—not right away. Then, late one night in December 2017, I was lying in bed, watching *Stranger Things*. The Netflix series was an instant favorite of mine when it came out in the summer the year before, and I was binging season two. I took a video of myself talking about the latest season and posted it to my story on Instagram. A short time later, Tia left a reply.

"Oh my God, I love El," she wrote. "The show is amazing, isn't it?"

I responded immediately.

"Yeah, it's great."

I never heard from Becca or Lauren, but Tia and I DMed each other. We exchanged numbers and texted fast and furiously throughout the day and night. It didn't seem like either of us slept. Two days later, I FaceTimed with her. I couldn't believe that we were doing this. It seemed crazy. Tia was a physical therapist from small-town Arkansas. Her outgoing personality and her full laugh filled up the small screen on my phone.

She was fun and there was no end to all that we had to say to each other. I decided to let her know the reason I'd followed her.

"I have to be honest with you," I said.

I saw her tense.

"What do you mean?" she asked.

I explained I was being considered for the next season of *The Bachelorette*, which was how I came to find and follow her, along with Becca and Lauren, though neither of them had responded to my requests. She was thrown off at first, and understandably so, but after giving the situation some thought she said, "Okay, cool. I'm good with it if you're good with it." Everybody was a player. It was game on. And soon she was dishing her thoughts on who was likely to be the next Bachelorette—or not be it.

This was dangerous territory, especially if her thoughts turned out to be correct. I knew we shouldn't be talking in the event I also ended up on the show. But that line had already been crossed, hadn't it? Tia agreed there was no reason to stop. The damage had been done. Since we lived in different parts of the country, the chances of us getting together outside the show were practically zero. What was the harm in continuing to text and talk?

On New Year's Eve, Tia and I FaceTimed with each other. Seeing her pop up on the screen was exciting and fun. I smiled broadly. She was partying with Lauren, one of Arie's finalists and the woman everyone expected him to give an engagement ring to. Then he stunned all of Bachelor Nation, not to mention Lauren herself, by proposing to Becca. But like Tia, Lauren looked in fine spirits, completely recovered and ready for a rebound when she popped into Tia's screen and said hi to me. *Happy New Year!*

The girls were whooping it up together—and good for them. I wished I could transport myself through the phone and be there with them. It seemed like a fun way to usher in the new calendar. Champagne and a flip of the page. Then something seemed to flip in the room there. Tia looked away from our conversation. She was distracted by something off to the side. The picture on the phone changed. Suddenly I was looking at the ceiling, then the sofa, and then Tia's leg and foot.

"What's going on?" I asked.

She repositioned the phone so I could see her again.

"Lauren's acting weird," she said.

"What do you mean?"

"I can't tell. She's over there . . . whatever."

"What do you mean whatever?"

It killed me to not know what was going on in that room. Tia reassured me that if it was something big, she'd tell me and we'd all know soon enough. As it turned out, we all would know soon enough. It was a huge change of heart. Until then, though, I had to be patient. Tia and I went back to flirting and laughing. Our conversation flitted all over the place until we wished each other a new year full of happiness, smiles, and good news.

In mid-January, the good news arrived. I received an email informing me that I had made it through to the final round of casting for season fourteen of *The Bachelorette*. "Congratulations," the note began. It provided details about travel and meetings, along with a reminder to make sure my cell phone was charged. "A handler will either call you or text you when you land," it said. Very cool, I thought. The interview was scheduled to take place a couple of days before my birthday. Would it be an early present?

I also received my settlement check from the Oakland Raiders.

Funny how the universe conspires to open doors and change your outlook all at the same time.

Since I was no longer broke, I decided to splurge for my birthday. I rented an Airbnb in Los Angeles and invited Tia to stay with me for a long weekend following my interview. I confided my plans to my friend Mike Zimmer, who said, "Dude, I always knew you'd end up on one of those reality dating shows." My dad worried when he heard about my plans with Tia and warned me to be careful.

"That's not how it's supposed to happen," he said.

I laughed. How did he know?

"It's the power of social media," I said.

Was he right? Yes. Was I trying to scheme a little? Yes. If Tia was going to be the Bachelorette, I wanted a head start on all the other guys. I knew the importance of preparing for a big game, and all I was really doing was preparing. I wanted to get to know Tia in person and let her get to know me better. Maybe we'd even really like each other.

I think Tia had similar thoughts. Both of us were playing a game, trying to figure out our next moves and have some fun in the process. What was the harm in that?

Happy Birthday

Once in LA, I checked into a hotel near the airport. I had an awesome workout the next morning before my pickup to burn off my nervousness. After a long, rejuvenating shower, I put on a white T-shirt and jeans with a bomber jacket. I also carried a blazer and button-down shirt on a hanger in case I needed a dressier change of clothes for an on-camera interview.

At the show's production office, several folks in casting met me in front and gave me a nice welcome. They ribbed me for bringing extra wardrobe. I laughed but felt no embarrassment. They knew I was taking this seriously.

I entered the room where I would be interviewed on camera and I met my producer. Everyone on *The Bachelorette* or *The Bachelor* gets assigned a producer, someone who ushers you through the process, answers questions, holds your hand, asks questions about what you think, how you feel, what else you're thinking and feeling, and more questions, and makes sure you feel comfortable. My producer introduced herself as Charlie Frank. She was a dark-haired hipster. Her hair was tied with a blue bandanna and she wore a cool printed T-shirt and torn, faded jeans. A pair of aviator sunglasses were on the table next to her notes and phone.

I liked her right away. At the same time, I thought, *Uh-oh*.

Charlie had been Tia's producer. She had told me all about her. She said she was super cool. "She's awesome," Tia had said. "She was there for me. She's my girl. I love Charlie. Be nice to her if you see her. *But don't tell her that you know me.*"

I told Charlie everything but that as she fired questions at me for the next hour and a half. There was one glaring omission to her interrogation: She never asked about my relationship with Aly. I am sure they knew about it. A Google search would have turned up stories and pictures. She didn't ask about Tia, either. A semi-careful check of our social media accounts would have revealed that we followed each other. I always wondered if they knew. In any event, after every question had been asked, Charlie knew a helluva lot about me.

Afterward, she took me into another conference room to meet, as she said, some of her friends. I walked in and there were all the show's producers, a group of several dozen people. They had been watching my interview on a large TV screen behind me. Charlie motioned toward a chair and suggested I make myself comfortable as the group had a few more questions they wanted to ask.

More questions?

I thought this was when they would for sure ask about Aly and Tia, but no, they didn't ask about either of them or try anything tricky. They focused on football—the highlights of my career and the low points. When they asked why I'd stopped playing, I pulled my shirt back and showed them the scars on my shoulder. Several people winced when I described the way bone chips had slipped from my collarbone and down into my pecs. They asked if I had any special talents. That made me laugh. No, I didn't. They asked me to describe a fantasy date, where in the world I wanted to travel, and what a hometown date might include.

The only curve ball I got came from a producer with unruly, long brown hair and a scraggly hipster beard. His personality matched his appearance: wild and creative. Smiling, scratching his head like a hippie detective or the lead singer of the Spin Doctors, he said he was intrigued by my lack of dating history and he must've had a hunch about something because he got straight to the point in a way no one else had managed to do after hours of questioning.

"What's your number?" he said.

I smiled and took a breath before answering. I'd received media training from the NFL and knew the basics of sitting up straight, being aware of my camera angle, and, most important, taking a moment to gather my thoughts before answering a tough question. Never let your emotions dictate your response.

He asked more directly: How many girls had I slept with?

I remembered being asked the same question when I was with the Chargers. "I'll just say this," I said. "I can count the girls I've slept with on one hand."

Another producer in the room asked how I felt about kissing and making out with cameras pointed at me and a production crew watching, and later eight million people tuning in on TV and talking about it on social media. Good question. Like a lot of these questions, I hadn't thought of them until I was asked, or if I had, I hadn't thought about them in depth, and this one cut right to the heart of the show. How much of myself was I willing to reveal? How far were you willing to go? Emotionally? Physically? Romantically?

Marriage?

I tilted my head and looked up at the ceiling, as if the answers were somewhere up in the tiles. They weren't. They were inside me. This whole adventure was and would continue to be about addressing the things that made me uncomfortable. I was ready to put them behind me—and in front of the whole country. Which made me laugh. How bizarre, right?

I said as much, too. I was used to playing football in front of people, and I was chill about kissing on camera. I was willing to open my heart and also risk heartbreak if that happened. I could handle it. "I'm ready to go and have a good time," I said.

But not so fast.

Someone had another question: "What are your thoughts on who you'd like to see become the next bachelorette?"

I was ready for that one, too.

"I've read some spoilers," I said. "Based on those, I like Lauren, Tia, and Becca. Those are my three."

I saw people in the room nod.

"All three are great girls," the producer said.

Then I was finished. As I got up and the room began to clear, someone asked what I was doing to celebrate my birthday. As they knew from all the forms I'd filled out and even something I'd said, the next day, Friday, was my twenty-sixth birthday. I was staying out in LA, I said. My mom was coming out, and we were going to enjoy the city. I wonder how they would've reacted if I'd told them what I really had planned.

From there, I went straight to my Airbnb in Hollywood. Tia arrived later that night, and we cooked a delicious birthday dinner together. She was ready to have a good time, and so was I. The next day we hiked up Runyon Canon and took in the panoramic views of Hollywood from the top of that mountain. She also surprised me with a bouquet of balloons that said, "Happy Birthday Mother-fucker."

The only awkwardness in this long weekend sleepover came when we were in bed together that first night. We were making out and Tia rolled on top of me, indicating she was ready to go to the next level or two or three. I revealed my v-card and said, "No, we're good." Tia was surprised but totally cool and respectful. It was altogether different than my similar experience in high school. She gave me a kiss, got up and showered, and then we went to sleep.

By the time we said goodbye, our long weekend together was exactly as I'd intended: three days packed with fun activities and nonstop conjecture between two people obsessed with who was going to be cast on the next season of *The Bachelorette*. Tia was convinced I was going to make it onto the show. Aware of the twist with Lauren and Arie, she was sure Becca was going to be tapped as the Bachelorette. That bummed her out, but she remained hopeful, and as we kissed goodbye, she said, "All we can do is see what happens."

If You Don't End Up with Becca, I'll See Your Ass in Paradise

I was eager to get some insider gossip when I FaceTimed with Tia and found her vacationing in Fort Lauderdale with Becca and Caroline Lunny, another *Bachelor* participant whom Arie had eliminated in week four.

"Girl's trip," Tia said, with a playful smile.

She had me say hi to Becca and Caroline. Even on the small screen of my phone I could tell they were having fun in the sun. Three beautiful young women, their moods upbeat and in party mode. Tia explained that I was the guy she'd told them about. Then her face filled the screen and her voice was quieter, more intimate as she confided in me. Sensing Becca was going to be the next Bachelorette, she was feeling down.

"I would want it to be you," I told her, as a measure of support. "But if I'm picked and you aren't, I'm still going to do the show."

She understood.

"I would want you to," she said. "It was a great experience for me. I would want you to have the same thing. If it's offered, go for it."

I didn't know when I might hear, and as I waited, I began to have doubts and concerns. It was typical of me. I got scared or nervous and wondered if I should back out. It was no different from when I was invited to parties back in high school and college. It was easier to say no. It was safer is what it was. There were no risks. Of course, there were also no rewards.

Was I crazy for wanting to do this?

I hadn't ever even signed up for a dating app.

What business did I have trying to date, fall in love, and get engaged all at once on TV? It was a recipe for failure or foolishness or both. Why bother?

I got mad at myself.

Why not bother? The best time of my life had been spending time with Aly. Why not try to find someone else?

But on TV? Really?

This debate raged in my head. In the meantime, now that I wasn't broke anymore, I got out of my dad's basement. I signed a yearlong lease on an apartment just outside of Denver proper and made plans to get some furniture. Then, on a Saturday morning, I heard the ping of an email arriving, and with it, my life changed.

February 24, 2018

Dear Colton,

Congratulations! You have been selected to be part of ABC's prime time series, The Bachelorette.

I have attached a congratulatory letter and packing lists for your review. Please give Lacy a call to go over the packing lists and she will answer any questions you have.

Please reply to this email in order to confirm it was received. Thank you for your patience and

*cooperation throughout this process. We will make
this official when we receive your signed agreement.*

Have a nice weekend.

Have a nice weekend. Now that was funny.

The next two weeks raced past in a blur of excitement and anticipation. I felt like I'd been traded to the Patriots, only this was better. I didn't want to kiss Tom Brady, but I was certain I'd want to make out with the Bachelorette if given the chance. There was a lot to do and get ready before I left.

I signed and returned the show's agreement, as requested. Then I went through the extensive packing list that included driver's license and passport, one "gorgeous suit for the first night" (ideally two or more), slacks and dress shirts, casual evening clothes, casual day clothes, workout clothes, comfortable travel attire for possible long-haul flights, coats and jackets, winter hat, gloves and boots, pants and shirts, all types of shoes, T-shirts, swim trunks of course, and slippers if desired. Also: sunglasses (worn off-camera only) and sunscreen, prescription medications, personal items including skin care products, body and hair products, and anything else I couldn't live without.

The last line made me laugh. My daily attire typically ranged from a T-shirt and sweatpants to more T-shirts and sweatpants. But I got it. The stuff I packed had to last up to three months—that is, if things went well. It also had to work anywhere in the world. Potential locations weren't revealed beforehand. Oh, everything had to fit into two suitcases, leaving just enough room for an engagement ring!

To that end, we were instructed to delete and disconnect ourselves from any dating apps and set all of our social media accounts to private, which I did. Finally, with the checklist complete, the real fun began.

I partnered with a producer named Ruby and a crew from LA on my introductory video, the brief profile that would give the viewers a sense of where I came from and who I was in real life. They shot me in various locations around Denver: Children's Hospital (where I did my third AffloVest giveaway), walking Sniper, tossing a football with my dad, and relaxing in my new condo. I was very grateful I'd gotten my own place. My dad's basement would not have been a good first impression.

The shoot concluded with a sit-down interview. After this long, fun day, I looked forward to answering Ruby's questions. Like so many of the producers I would meet, she was sharp, outgoing, and quick-witted, someone who ingratiated herself quickly and had a quality that made you want to be her friend. Only one subject was off-limits in our interview: my relationship with Aly. She'd confronted Larry Nassar in court and the reasons I didn't want to talk about her were obvious. The show respected that request.

Ruby could've asked about two other sensitive issues, both of them potentially explosive topics: Tia and my virginity. But she didn't know about either of them, and I vowed to keep them private. People didn't need to know *everything*.

By March, I was counting the days until my flight left for LA. It's all I talked about to family and friends. My dad was nervous but wanted me to have a good time. My mom wished me luck but didn't like the show. Coach Nowinsky said his wife was a superfan of the show who struggled to reconcile the image of the young guy who used to sit at their dinner table going on her favorite TV program, but he added, "She'll want to know everything."

With just a couple of days to go, I got a call from a woman in casting. I was getting my teeth cleaned when she called. She chuckled at my attention to detail.

"I'm going to send you a final checklist," she said. "I want to make sure you're packed."

"I'm all set," I said.

"You'll get here, and you'll go straight into the show."

"I'm ready."

"Remember your passport," she said. "Seriously, don't forget it. And we'll see you in a few days."

I spent the next day making a final round of calls to family and friends. My best friend Mike wished me luck. My brother simply said, "Try to get laid." Finally, from the airport, my last call went to Tia. I'd already told her that I was going on the show, but I wanted one more pep talk from her.

"Just have fun and be yourself," she said. "Becca is an amazing person. And if you don't end up with her, I'll see your ass in paradise."

We're Here for Survivor, Right?

PART I: SEQUESTRATION

With all the things I could've been thinking about on the two-and-a-half-hour flight to Los Angeles from Denver, I couldn't stop thinking about Tia and my virginity. They were my only two secrets, and both worried me. I saw Tia as a potential reason the show's producers might kick me off the show before it even started. With her, I'd meddled in areas that, while not explicitly forbidden, seemed like they'd be disqualifiers if they were known.

And as for being a virgin, I knew it ran counter to the image I projected as a twenty-six-year-old former pro football player, which might be a good thing. But I also feared it could be seen as too much of a responsibility for the Bachelorette, and therefore a reason I might not get very far when the roses were handed out.

I fixated on these the whole flight—and it wasn't like I hadn't already spent considerable time thinking about these things before getting on the plane.

I vowed again and again and again to keep these a secret.

Good luck, Mr. Harrison.

No chance, Becca.

Then the plane landed, and I told myself that I was officially done thinking about these things. Just like football. Put the nagging little injuries out of mind, run on the field, and have a good time. I claimed my two bags and hooked up with my driver. An hour later, he deposited me at a nice hotel, Westlake Village. There, a welcoming production coordinator met me in the lobby and offered a large, empty envelope with my name on it.

"Put your phone and your charger inside," she said. "And any other devices you might have—iPad, computer."

"Just my phone," I said, as I watched her seal the envelope.

I located my room and stayed there for the next three days. A producer kept me company during the day and we got to know each other pretty well. I missed my phone, laptop, and iPad. Without texts, email, and social media, I suffered information withdrawal. Seriously. I went from checking my devices fifty or sixty times a day, as most people do, to zero. Just totally cold turkey. And it was insanely hard.

The other guys went through the same process as they arrived. I scheduled gym time and worked out without running into anyone else, which was obviously intentional but also unfortunate. I was interested in checking out the competition. My room was on the first floor and from the balcony, I was right across from the pool and hot tub. On my second day there, the temptation of that hot tub was too great to resist. I was going stir-crazy.

I watched it all afternoon and evening and waited until well past midnight before sneaking outside and slipping into the hot water. I don't think I actually said anything, but the sound of immediate pleasure in my head was so loud I was afraid others heard it. I leaned back and stared up at the stars in the mostly clear sky. It was the most perfect hot tub ever—that is until I was hit by a wave of paranoia.

I panicked. What if they saw me? What if they caught me breaking the rules? I didn't want to get sent home before the dang thing had started. I hoisted myself out of the water in a single motion and quickly snuck back inside, dripping water but undetected.

All I had to do was hang in there one more day.

PART II: THE FREAK-OUT

Finally, the big day arrived. We were going to meet Becca. We were going to make first impressions. Some of us would get roses. Others wouldn't. It was all very exciting to say the least, and reminiscent of bouncing around in the tunnel in the final moments before a big game. Nervous energy took over. But not so fast. Shooting wouldn't start until it was dark, and it would last through the night. I—and the twenty-nine other guys—were advised to rest.

I had brought two nice outfits for this first night at the Bachelor mansion, a blue tux and a navy suit with some red detail in the pattern. I chose the tux and went with an open collar rather than a tie. I hated wearing ties. My producer told me that my makeup person was on her way and then I would get mic'd for the night. I nodded and pretended to look cool and calm, but I was anything but cool and calm.

I was hit by a sudden attack of nervous anxiety. Damn it, I thought, why is this happening now? My mind was spiraling out of control. The motherboard was on the fritz and throwing everything else out of whack. I had trouble catching my breath. My face turned a ghostly white. I was about to look at myself in the mirror but decided to sit down in a chair instead and try to center myself. My producer asked if I was all right.

"No, I need to talk to Ruby," I said, referring to his boss, my main producer.

He got her on his phone and handed it to me.

"Ruby, can you come by my room?" I asked.

"Yeah, sure," she said. "Is everything okay?"

"I have to talk to you," I said.

I was still in the chair when she arrived. Her energy level was running as high as expected of someone heavily invested and involved in the first night of production on one of TV's highest-rated reality series. It was showtime! As for me, I was, to put it bluntly, freaking out. My heart was beating like it wanted to escape and my breathing was equally fast and hard to control. I'm sure my face was a billboard for all this anxiety because Ruby sat down next to me, gave my shoulder a squeeze, and told me that everything was going to be okay. She was a professional problem solver, and I had a problem.

"Something's bothering me," I said.

"I can see," she said. "Do you want to tell me about it?"

"Yes. But I don't want it to cause a problem."

"I'm sure it won't," she said. "Let's hear it. Go."

I had to tell her what was bothering me. My promise to keep my secrets secret wasn't working. I was crumbling under the weight of my own inclination to tell the truth. And so I made a last-minute confession to Ruby. I knew Tia. I explained how we met on social media and spent the weekend together after my final round of casting in LA. I also told her that while FaceTiming with Tia about three weeks earlier, I'd met Becca. They were on a girls getaway in Florida, I explained, adding that our introduction had been so fast I could barely remember it.

"We didn't say much more than hello," I said.

Ruby listened without showing any emotion. No surprise, no anger, no curiosity. When I was done, she merely said, "Thank you." That was it? Thank you? Her response did nothing to help my anxiety or calm my paranoia. Then again, my ass was the one in front of the camera, not hers.

That did nothing to soothe my anxiety.

"I want to at least brace production for it in case my first meeting with Becca goes south or gets awkward," I said.

"Don't worry," she said. "Take a breath. There's nothing you can do."

"What do you mean?"

"When you have your first conversation, you'll know if she recognizes you."

She didn't seem upset. I took that as a sign I wasn't going to get kicked off the show at the last minute, which by itself was a huge relief. My breathing returned to normal, and ever so gradually, so did the rest of me. After standing up, Ruby squeezed my shoulder again and assured me I was going to be okay.

I hoped it would be.

PART III: LET'S GET THIS PARTY POPPIN'

The sun was beginning to set in a sky streaked with pinks, oranges, and yellows, when my producer escorted me into the hotel lobby. There, I finally saw several of the other guys. Before I could introduce myself to anyone, I was led to an open door at the back of an idling limo. Three guys were already inside: Jason Tartick, William "Wills" Reid, and Christon Staples. A producer and cameraman were also wedged toward the front. I slid in and smiled at everyone.

"This is for *Survivor*, right?" I said.

It was a perfect icebreaker. Everyone laughed and relaxed as much as possible given the situation. We shared friendly chitchat about how nuts it was that this was all really happening. Finally. A short time later we arrived at the gate of the 7,500-square-foot Mediterranean villa, a.k.a. The Mansion, and continued slowly up the driveway.

Conversation in the limo stopped. After months of interviews and prep, here we were—and this reality snapped us to attention.

All of us were silently reviewing the clever and cute lines we had worked up to greet Becca. We knew a good first impression was crucial in determining whether we would receive a rose or get sent home. Producers had reviewed our ideas and offered assistance where needed to ensure we had a unique and camera-friendly hello.

I'd wanted to walk up to Becca with a local rescue dog and explain that both of us were hoping to find someone who'd fall in love with us. But Blake was riding in on an ox—to show his love was as strong as an ox—and so producers asked me to come up with another idea. Unable to come up with anything I liked as much as my initial idea, I settled for little party poppers that literally popped and released a spray of confetti. I planned to give one to Becca and say, "Let's get this party poppin'!"

I'd rehearsed my line a thousand times and was still rehearsing it in my head as I watched Jason, Wills, and Christon take their turns meeting Becca. I took it all in—their confident walks to Becca, their smiles, their cute dances, the way they gave Becca a respectful peck on the cheek. That this was really happening seemed crazy and surreal.

I managed to block my fear that Becca might recognize me. If it happened? Well, then it would happen. It was too overwhelming to even consider.

Breathe.

Deep breaths.

Then I was up. Just a crack, and the show's stage manager, Paul "Big Paulie" Danner, leaned into the back and gave me final instructions. Six feet three inches tall, with a polished bald pate and a body that had muscles on top of muscles, Paulie was either the scariest or the friendliest guy on the set. He filled a number of roles, including bouncer, big brother, steadying presence, and field general. He made sure everyone followed instructions and kept on schedule.

"So here's the deal," he began, before pausing after seeing the faraway look in my eyes. "You okay?"

"Yup. Fine. Just freaking out a little."

"Great. So here's the deal. The driver is going to come around and open the door for you. You're going to take a step out and button your tux. The door will close behind you. Don't look behind you. Take a breath. Then you'll walk up, you'll see your mark, stand on your mark, you'll see Becca, and then you'll make your introduction. Got it?"

"Sounds easy enough," I said.

"Any questions?"

"Yeah, what am I doing again?"

PART IV: A LOT OF GOOD-LOOKING DUDES

I have no memory of introducing myself to Becca. I watched it later on TV, and it seemed to go well. Otherwise, my brain is missing that chunk of time. I swear I blacked out as soon as Paulie gave me the cue to get out of the car and go. Despite all the hours I'd spent rehearsing, I still fumbled my one line. On the bright side, I didn't trip. I didn't say, "Let's get this party pooping." And Becca didn't recognize me. Success!

The next thing I remember, I was walking into the mansion's living room and finding it packed with a bunch of guys, all magnificently coiffed, dressed, and spritzed with cologne. Everybody shined. The room buzzed with a nervous, hypercompetitive energy. Realizing I still had the expended popper in my hand, I casually ditched it behind the door, and as soon as I did, one guy said, "Hey, what'd you just put over there?"

"My prop," I said. "The thing I used to say hello to Becca."

"What'd you do?" someone else asked from across the room.

Everyone was on edge. There was nothing to do until Becca

finished meeting all the guys. Then our one-on-ones would begin. I looked around the room and thought, *Holy shit, there are a lot of good-looking dudes here*. It was intimidating. But I managed to calm down and even enjoy meeting some of the guys. I'd already won a small victory. Becca hadn't recognized me. Or she played it cool and didn't say anything if she did. I had no recollection other than that I made it through our first hello without incident.

Our first one-on-one also went by without any acknowledgment of our previous FaceTime. If she remembered me, she didn't show it. Neither did I remind her. It would've made for good television, but an early exit, too. I kept small talk to my NFL career and the satisfaction I got from my foundation. I hit my bullet points. I thought Becca looked amazing. We seemed to connect. I was good.

Or so I thought. It was close to 4:00 a.m. when I got my first rose. I was off in a corner by myself, the first alone time I'd had in hours. I was trying to process all that had just happened—something nearly impossible due to the constant demands of production. There was never enough downtime. I hoped I had made as good of a first impression on Becca as she had on me, when I heard my producer Ruby's voice.

"Let's talk for a minute," she said.

"Sure, what's up?" I said.

We backed away from the group.

"Hey, I know you asked me not to tell anyone about the thing with you and Tia, but I think we should loop in somebody else."

I looked down at the floor and chuckled to myself. I was too tired to panic. If she'd told other people, I had to go with it. I trusted her.

"Okay, fine," I said.

Ruby motioned for senior producer Michael Finn—everyone called him Finnster—to join us. He'd been hanging nearby, probably waiting for her to signal him. The three of us went into a nearby room. At Ruby's prompting, I told Finnster that I'd contacted Tia on social media, spent a weekend with her, and met Becca over FaceTime a few weeks prior to production. I expressed relief that Becca hadn't seemed to remember.

Finnster listened with the impassive, interested expression of a doctor. I couldn't tell if he was surprised, but he was definitely paying attention.

"You might want to mention it the next time you see Becca," he said.

"Sure, if you think that's cool."

"We'll leave it up to you."

In Way Over My Head

T he sun was up when we wrapped the first rose ceremony. Exhausted, cranky, aching to get into bed, we climbed aboard shuttles and returned to our hotel. I was one of the few guys who wasn't still holding on to his rose. I was never sentimental about them, unlike some of the other guys. After a few hours of sleep, we climbed back aboard the shuttles, this time with our bags, and moved into the mansion.

All of us were assigned roommates. Mine were Blake Horstmann, Garrett Yrigoyen, David Ravitz, and John Graham. They took the two bunk beds, while I claimed a single bed off to the side, though I had to stack my two suitcases at the end so my feet wouldn't hang over the edge.

As I unpacked and looked around the mansion, I thought about the guy Becca had eliminated before the rose ceremony, Jake Enyeart. They'd met several times in the past. While it turned out there was nothing wrong or against the rules about that, she wondered why he was interested in her now when he hadn't shown any interest before. Was he wasting her time? Was he being an opportunist and using her?

She didn't wait for answers. She got rid of him.

Would that be my fate, too? Would I receive similar treatment when our previous encounter was brought up, as I knew it would be?

These questions and others weighed on my mind all day as we shot our group date playing trampoline dodgeball and then changed clothes for our group-date cocktail party. I was amazed at the way one tiny spark of concern could erupt into major paranoia. I didn't want to go home this soon. I'd told everyone I could be gone up to three months. Returning after four days would be embarrassing. I'd have to explain what happened—or didn't happen.

I obsessed over whether I should say something or keep my mouth shut. I tried to think through every angle and possibility, and in the end, there was only one option: the truth. When it was my turn to talk with Becca, I told her about my friendship with Tia. I was straightforward and matter-of-fact, as is my style. I said it started on social media, included a lot of texting and FaceTime, and one weekend together.

But that was history, as far as I was concerned, and a brief one at best. I had nothing to hide. I assured Becca that I thought she was an awesome person who I really wanted to get to know, and I hoped she might feel similarly about me.

I saw Ruby and Finnster watching us from the side, looking pleased with my end of the conversation. I felt good about it, too. I'd said my piece clearly and confidently. How Becca would react was anyone's guess. That's something I came to love and fear about these shows. For all the production and planning, no one knew what people would actually say or the way others would react.

"It makes me feel a little bit sick," Becca responded, before going off to think about what she wanted to do. I assumed that she had spoken with Tia and already knew her version of the backstory. It was up to her how she wanted to deal with it. She didn't rush to a decision. Later, at the cocktail party, we had our next encounter and she was still undecided.

The drama was drawn out until the rose ceremony.

I got a rose.

I was relieved.

But I went to sleep that night aware that I'd still be in the danger zone when I woke up, and I was. The next day began with a group date. I was one of six guys tapped to accompany Becca and five of her friends to a spa and pamper them with foot massages and pedicures. It was a fun, sexy idea, but I had a hunch that something else was up. Just before we went into the salon to meet our so-called clients, I huddled to the side with Jason.

"I think I figured out something," I said. "Becca is going to be joined on this group date by some of her friends, and I'm sure Tia will be among them. I have a history with her. If things get sticky, you gotta help me out."

I wondered if I was being paranoid. Was I overthinking everything? No, I wasn't. My paranoia turned out to be an accurate premonition. When we walked in, Becca was flanked by her friends, all of them wearing white terry-cloth bathrobes, and there, to her left, was Tia. I was so nervous. Tia looked great—and from what I could see, she was way more relaxed than me. I didn't get any vibe from Becca.

Jason understood, though. As he said, Becca might not be able to see me as anything other than her friend's ex. All of us guys changed into spa attendant uniforms and returned to the salon. Before we entered, though, I asked the guys for a favor. "I'm going to go in last and I need one of you to sit in front of Tia. Don't leave her for me."

They nodded, like *of course, bro*, but when I got in and looked for an empty spot, the only one available was in front of my friend Tia.

"So everything's going well?" she asked.

I didn't know how much to tell her or even what to say. I didn't want to tell her about my relationship with Becca, but I also have a hard time saying anything but the truth. I don't lie, and if I tried,

I knew Tia would see through it and bust me. No thanks, not on national TV. I smiled and moved forward.

"I'm here now and giving this an opportunity," I said.

"I wouldn't want to take the opportunity from you," she said. "Explore it. See if she's the one for you. If she is, awesome, I'll be happy for you."

I saw Becca later that day and asked if she and Tia had a good catch-up at the spa. She played it really cool.

"I'll tell you about it later," she said.

As she walked away, I took a deep breath and sighed. I was only four days into this thing and knew I was in over my head. How did I not know this before? There were too many moving parts to keep track of. I was up against masters. What saved me was Becca herself. I knew the final decision as to who got a rose belonged to her, not the producers, and I got a good vibe from Becca. I sensed that she was playing the game, but also that she really liked me.

I reminded myself to be as authentic as possible in every situation. Even at this early stage, I sensed the temptation to play a game and think that you could outsmart the process and the producers, and I knew that was the wrong move. As in any relationship, the show was about letting someone see your real self, not just your best self.

I really did want to fall in love.

Would it be with Becca?

I thought it might be when I saw her later that night at the soiree that followed all group dates. Since the spa day had gone well, I wanted to put the whole Tia thing safely behind us and begin writing our own story. I knew only one sure way to do that: I had to kiss Becca. As I waited for her to enter the party, I worked out a plan in my head. If I saw her smiling when it was time for our private chat, I was going to give her a kiss before either of us said a word. Pretty bold, I thought, but it would make a statement and serve as a clear reboot of our situation.

If she wasn't smiling . . .

Once she got in front of me, I couldn't tell. Her expression was impossible to read. If I looked any harder, my nose would have been pressing against her forehead. She had a world-class poker face. As we sat down next to each other, she appeared to offer multiple expressions, as if fucking with me: first, a faint smile; then a subtle frown that seemed to convey disappointment; and then her expression changed again, like she was getting ready to discipline me. It was like trying to read three different foreign languages without understanding any of them. The worst part? She didn't say anything. Her silence killed me. Is there any weapon sharper?

I wanted her to say something. Anything.

Or to just smile again.

It's amazing how fast the mind can create a thousand different scenarios, all of them worse than the previous one.

She had to already know everything, I thought. She and Tia had spent time together, so obviously she knew everything. But suddenly I wanted to make sure. I wanted to explain that Tia and I were just friends. I also had an overwhelming urge to tell her everything else about myself: that I loved my dog, that my parents' divorce had messed me up, that I'd once looked at gay porn, that my favorite drink was sangria, that I'd binge-watched *Friends* . . . whatever she wanted to know, I was an open book. I was willing to confess to anything.

Finally, she broke out in a big grin. I couldn't tell if she looked like she might be about to laugh, but she looked like she was messing with me, and enjoying every minute that I squirmed nervously across from her. I didn't care. We had a good talk, an even better kiss, and I knew things between us were going to be okay.

Another Short List

Some quick notes on that season:

1. Late at night following the after-party, David, one of my four roommates, was rushed to the hospital after rolling out of his top bunk and crashing to the ground. I'd gone to bed earlier than the other guys, but the noise of his fall woke me up. I saw David lying on the floor, seizing and spitting up blood. Blake was on top of him, trying to help, while yelling for producers since none of us had cell phones. Fortunately, David recovered.

2. Yes it was weird making out with someone I knew might also be kissing one, two, or maybe ten other guys that same day. Before group dates, I always asked production if I could be the first guy to talk to Becca so I didn't feel like I was getting seconds, thirds, or sixths when we kissed.

3. Making out in front of cameras, producers, makeup people, and others on the crew was weird.

4. Even weirder, I got used to it. Even though this small army of people stood only a few feet away, it was like I didn't see them anymore.

5. Bathrooms in the mansion were shared. Every morning and especially when we returned after a long day of shooting on location, there was a race—literally a race—to the bathrooms.

6. It was also a free-for-all in the kitchen. In the morning, guys got up at all different hours and made their own breakfast. I usually fixed myself eggs. Dinner was more often than not a group dinner. Both Wills and I loved to cook, and one night he made bacon-wrapped lamb and I cooked a side of Brussels sprouts.

7. The dishwasher was broken all season. All the dishes had to be hand-washed. We had a rule: if you cooked for the group, you didn't have to do dishes.

8. On the nights we had rose ceremonies, the show catered dinner.

9. For groceries, we wrote our requests in a notebook and submitted them to our producers. No one asked for caviar, but we ate well: steaks, salmon, and chicken.

10. When you're a contestant, you don't see or hear from Chris Harrison. He wasn't there to hang or chill with the guys. If Chris was there, something was about to go down.

Why Not Just Say It?

The next morning I sat down with my two producers, Ruby and Robbie, to talk about my one-on-one with Becca. It was the usual buzz of questions and conversation that work friends might have after a big day, except it was on camera. But it was nothing like an interrogation or interview. They asked questions and I talked my way through until it felt like we were all on the same page: I was in good standing with Becca. Maybe even better than good.

Then Robbie excused himself and left me alone with Ruby, who kept the conversation going in such an easy manner that I barely noticed I was talking about Tia again. Ruby was that smooth. She was Dr. Freud in a T-shirt and jeans—and much more pleasant to look at than an old Austrian man with a beard and a cigar. She told some stories about her own relationship before gently and effortlessly guiding me back onto Tia.

"I thought we were past her," I said. "What more can I say?"

Lighthearted and curious, she wanted to know more about the weekend I spent with Tia. She expressed surprise that we spent two nights together without doing anything more than making out. I understood her reaction and also her desire to know more and figure out the mystery behind it. Kind of like a Rubik's Cube. Tia and I liked each other. We were attracted to each other. We were single. We were in bed together. And yet . . . *How do these pieces fit together? Can you show me?*

Because I was talking to Ruby and we had a rapport, I admitted that I didn't have much experience in that department. I saw no downside to being honest. The truth never hurts, and it's much easier to go through life without hiding anything. But . . . oh crap, I realized that I *was* hiding something. I started the show with two secrets. One was already out and the other was on its way to being hung out in public like a load of laundry. As much as I liked Ruby, I didn't want to go there. I really didn't. I knew if I admitted . . . I just really, truly didn't want to say I was a virgin. And then I said it.

I should have a warning tattooed on my forehead: Secrets are not safe with me, especially my own secrets.

Beyond asking a few questions, Ruby was cool about it, in that way someone is when they are accustomed to hearing all sorts of things about people, and she assured me that I didn't have to bring it up right away.

"I don't really want to bring it up at all," I said, thinking about my upcoming date with Becca.

She shrugged and said I didn't have to mention it.

And I didn't—not then, anyway.

Becca and I went to Las Vegas on our one-on-one date. It was week five, the midway point of the show, and I got excited when I heard the destination was Vegas. I thought of all the incredibly cool things we could do there. I'd been to Vegas a few times with friends and always had fun. I came up with a long list of possibilities: nightclub shows, concerts, fancy dinners, outrageous day clubs in hotel swimming pools, gambling, gondola rides, the High Roller observation wheel.

But instead of the epic and awesome possibilities I imagined, we were driven out into the middle of the desert, where we found two camels waiting for us. I didn't hear any humping jokes as we mounted our camels and rode them through the desert. And when we crossed the Virgin River? I kept my thoughts to myself. But I gave the show major props. Very clever. I had no doubt that sign would make it on-screen later, which it did.

Our camel ride ended when we came upon a *Bachelorette*-style oasis, a hot tub and a tray of chilled libations. Becca and I peeled off our clothes and slid into the water. The bubbles offered a soothing massage following our bumpy ride across the rocks and sand. Conversation was as brief as our swimsuits. Both of us were more interested in exploring our more obvious and irresistible physical attraction.

We rendezvoused again later that night for a romantic dinner. As expected, she asked about my past girlfriends. It was impossible to know how much she'd been briefed about me, but I assumed she knew more than I knew about her. I assured her that I was taking this opportunity at a relationship seriously even though I didn't have as many past girlfriends as some of the other guys on the show. I was just picky, I said.

After that long day, I returned to the mansion to find my virginity had turned into a hot topic gone viral within the house. Full disclosure: a week or two before Las Vegas, I had confided in my mansion-mates, Jason and Garrett, the two guys with whom I was closest. I don't know why I felt compelled to spill the tea on myself other than it was weighing heavily on my mind. I suppose I was testing the water.

Jason and Garrett both expressed surprise to hear I was still a virgin. It had been a long time since either one of them had heard the word associated with anything other than quality olive oil. But they were supportive. And talkative. Apparently they interpreted my "please don't tell anyone" as code for "tell everyone," and word traveled through the house like a rumor at a slumber party of twelve-year-old girls that someone had gone to first base.

"That's fucking awesome," one of my mansion-mates said. "I'm a sex addict. I have way too much. If these people knew how much I had, I wouldn't be on the show."

I guess we represented the extremes. The comments and wisecracks didn't bother me. What choice did I have? They said more about the person making them than they did anything about me. As I'd discovered in high school, sexual preference is not a choice. It may be confusing; there may be questions, fear, and embarrassment; and figuring it out may take some time, as well as some courage.

I suppose that's at the core of discovering your sexuality. Asking questions. Making choices. Experimentation. Finding your comfort zone and revealing your true, naked self through an act of love—with someone who will share in that experience and make you feel good about it, and about yourself. I'd chosen to stay a virgin until I fell in love. It started as an easy way to protect myself from something that scared me, and by the time I went on *The Bachelorette* it had evolved into a requirement: I needed to be in love with that person.

But that didn't mean I hadn't been intimate. Only that I hadn't done one of the countless things people did when they chose to get close and make each other feel good. I didn't think of that as a negative. Neither was it a reason to be ridiculed or shamed. When I heard someone say their number was six, fifteen, twenty-eight, or much higher than all those together, I didn't slut-shame them, envy all those hookups, or make jokes. Who was I to judge?

At the same time, I knew I was judged every time I admitted my virginity. You? A twenty-six-year-old former pro football player? WTF? What happened? LMAO! It was contrary to the image of a big, strong football player, but I was okay with not being a stereotype. Who wants to be a cardboard cutout? Those who got to know me discovered it was only one facet of me. It didn't define me. And it was, in fact, much less interesting than the work I did with my foundation. One act helped prolong life, the other lasted a few minutes.

The mistake would be to think that I didn't want to trade my v-card for a did-it-card. I just wanted to be in love when I did it. Not an easy precondition. Ask the forty million single Americans registered on dating apps. But that's why I was on *The Bachelorette*. I wanted to find that special person. I needed help.

Maybe the fact that I didn't make sex the defining issue of my masculinity made me more interesting to some people. Maybe they saw a twentysomething with layers of complexity. Maybe they saw a guy with the courage and conviction to walk his own path, despite sometimes feeling scared, not always sure of himself, vulnerable, and perhaps a little embarrassed. I refused to see any of these as negatives. All I could do was make choices that felt right for me, and that was truly the beginning and end of the story of my virginity.

If that made other people uncomfortable or compelled them to joke about it or look down on me, that was their problem. I was pretty sure such reactions only indicated they had yet to fill in all the missing pieces in their own life. No one had it all figured out, including all the great-looking guys in the mansion seemingly filled with self-confidence. Weren't all of us there because something—or someone—was missing from our lives?

Maybe Ruby was right. Why not just say it?

I agreed.

It was part of who I was. It might be a little embarrassing, but that would last only for as long as it took to say it. Becca would understand without passing judgment, like she did with Tia. Hey, it might even make me more interesting to her, more attractive. Either way, once I said it, we would move on. It couldn't possibly turn into a big deal, right?

"I Would Never Judge You . . . or Think Any Less of You for That"

Week six was spent in Richmond, Virginia, shooting an American history–themed episode that later aired just before the Fourth of July. I participated very little and instead stood on the sidelines watching Connor Obrochta and Lincoln Adim slug it out. Those two guys didn't mix well on camera or behind the scenes. It had been the same with Jordan Kimball and Jean Blanc a couple of weeks earlier. As long as Connor and Lincoln didn't affect me, I was happy to stand off to the side and be like, y'all do your thing.

I got the group date rose and chilled. Maybe too much. Before the actual rose ceremony, Becca canceled the cocktail party and everyone did their ITMs (in-the-moment interviews) to fill the time. We were shooting in an old mansion, and I went to the bathroom. I locked the door behind me. The toilet was in a water closet, and I locked that door, too. As I did, the handle fell off. I was trapped, with no way to escape. It was thirty minutes before they found me. Both locks had to be picked to get me out of there.

I went back out and explained why I might look a little, uh, flushed. But I had my rose, so they could give me all the crap they wanted. After the ceremony, I enjoyed some quality time with Becca. She liked to hang out after the roses were all handed out and shoot the shit. Oftentimes for her, the party was just starting then.

We were having a good time, and I thought we were clicking again when she was pulled for an interview. Then producers took Blake for his ITM. The gathering was breaking up, and I started talking to Jason in the hallway. A nearby door opened, and I saw something that I shouldn't have: as Blake was supposed to be doing his interview, Becca was sitting on his lap, and they were making out.

I nudged Jason and told him to turn around.

"Dude, that's not cool," I said.

"Whoa," he said. "I guess that's it. Game over."

We kept that bit of intel to ourselves as we headed to the Bahamas week seven for sun and warm-weather fun. At this point, I didn't care whether I was among Becca's top choices. I was in the Caribbean, and I loved it there. As a high school freshman, I vacationed with my family on Grand Cayman and had the best and worst time of my life.

The best part? The weather was perfect, the water was warm, and I spent hours on a Jet Ski and scuba diving. One day, after scuba diving with my brother and my grandfather, I went snorkeling on my own. I explored cool coral caves and swam among the bright, tropical fish: blue tangs, French grunts, and needlefish. By the time I returned to our condo, though, I had an intense itching down my back, which turned into the worst part of my life.

I scratched through dinner, and then back at the condo it progressed in the worst way from a bad itch into something excruciatingly painful. I must've rubbed up against some fire coral while swimming through the coral caves. After trying cold compresses, my parents spoke to a local doctor, who recommended an over-the-counter ointment at the pharmacy, and soon my mom was rubbing ping up against the boat's pontoons. We acknowledged it with our eyes and devilish smiles. It was an opportunity to get even more personal.

"I'm looking forward to meeting your family," she said.

It was a friendly, much-appreciated slip that let me know I was on her list for hometowns. Thank you, Becca. I was getting a rose later.

The pressure was off. I relaxed and opened up, too.

"I'm nervous to go back home," I said.

"Why?" she asked.

"I've talked about things on this show that my parents don't even know."

"Like what?"

"You'll find out," I said, holding back for the first time.

She didn't press for more, and we went back up on the boat and enjoyed the rest of the day together, seemingly pressed against each other. When we regrouped for dinner later that night, I continued to feel comfortable with her, and close, and she seemed to feel similarly. Our chemistry and the fun we had together was undeniable. I overheard her tell her producer, as was later shown on TV, "He could just pick me up and do whatever he wants to do."

Like admit he was still a virgin?

Becca sat opposite me looking elegant and sexy in a beautiful black cocktail dress, with her hair brushed to one side revealing a dangling earring that had a hypnotic effect on me. She had a cocktail in front of her, and I had a glass of white wine. I toasted our wonderful day together and let her know it was something I would cherish forever. But while I didn't want to spoil our special time, and hoped I wouldn't, I had something to tell her. "It's something I struggle with articulating," I said.

She took a deep breath, suddenly concerned. I continued, explaining I'd always put football ahead of everything, includit all over my back. It worked. My brother came in later as my mom was reapplying the cream.

"What's that?" he asked.

"Something the doctor recommended," my mom said.

Connor picked up the package and read the label.

"Vag-i-sil," he said. " 'Instant, long-lasting relief from intense itching. Fast-acting' . . . blah-blah-blah . . . 'specially designed for the, uh, *vaginal* area.' "

A faint smile crossed his face, like the Mona Lisa if she were about to say something naughty.

"Mom, aren't you putting it on the wrong place? Shouldn't you be rubbing that into Colt's vagina?"

The trip to Nassau was much better. Garrett and I shared a suite at a luxurious beachfront hotel and I had my second one-on-one date with Becca. Before I met up with her, Ruby suggested it might be time to tell Becca about my lack of, uh, experience. I'd been thinking the same thing. I wondered if Tia had already told her. Maybe they'd talked about it back in Fort Lauderdale. It didn't matter. I was ready for that conversation.

It was just a word. Only two syllables.

Vir. Gin.

No. Problem.

That afternoon, Becca and I went snorkeling. I was admiring her form underwater when we bobbed up beneath the large catamaran that had ferried us out to this most perfect diving spot. Becca was a lot of fun. I keep saying that because it's true. I remember gazing at her smile as we treaded water in the little area between the catamaran's pontoons and feeling like the tide was carrying my heart toward her. It was easy to enjoy her beauty and the sensuality of being with her in the water.

At some point we realized the crew was having a hard time hearing our audio above our kicks and splashes and the water lap-ing my personal life. "I haven't had that many girlfriends or dates because of sports, and because of that . . . uh, I still am a virgin."

The words came out of me in a halting manner. I sounded more nervous and embarrassed than I actually was. Don't get me wrong, revealing this most intimate part of my life to Becca was not easy, and I don't know why, but that word, *virgin*, had a strange kind of power that made it really hard to say even after I'd committed to telling her. Why was that? Everyone's a virgin up till some point. There's no rule about when you're supposed to give that up, not like at sixteen you can drive, at eighteen you can vote, at twenty-one you can drink, and . . .

Up till this moment, you could count the times I had talked about it on one hand: to my ex-girlfriend, Tia, the show's producers, several of the guys on the show, and a room full of NFL linebackers. As I told Becca, I wasn't even sure my dad knew. "It's something I'm proud of and something that everyone I see a future with should know," I said.

Becca excused herself from the table to sort through her thoughts. Obviously the show couldn't air every word of our conversation, but we had a long, thoughtful talk at the table, and she was receptive, sensitive, supportive, and respectful. I appreciated the way the show kept it so real. As I've said, it's all about confronting your truths. Becca assured me that she would never judge me for having made that personal decision. "I didn't expect to hear that from you, but it doesn't change my feelings," she said. "If anything, I respect you even more."

Producers interrupted us multiple times throughout dinner and pulled us away for our in-the-moment interviews. How do you feel? How do you think the talk went? What do you think is going through his/her mind? Robbie Watts, another producer assigned to me that night, wanted to know whether I was concerned Becca would send me home after what I'd just told her.

"She's not going to break up with me," I said.

"But what if she does? What if she's freaking out? What if it's just too much for her to deal with?"

"She'd be a really shallow person, and I know she's not. Becca is cool."

She was cool.

At the end of that long night, Becca gave me a rose and I returned to my room pleased with the outcome and believing the issue of my virginity was something I wouldn't have to deal with again on the show. I had four more days left in that tropical paradise with nothing to do but relax, swim, and avoid getting sunburned. Oh, and think about hometowns. It was a good trade-off.

As we wrapped in Nassau, though, something unexpected happened. Shit among all the remaining guys turned real. Everybody was falling for Becca and, whether it was a tone of voice or a blast of sarcasm, I could tell that jealousies were boiling just beneath the surface. We quit talking about Becca among ourselves. All of us had spent quality time with her and felt like we had a connection. It was impossible to spend time with Becca and not fall in love with her in some way, and those feelings were hard to share.

But were they shared? One night, Garrett let it slip that he and Becca had talked about her father. From seeing her on Arie's season, I knew that Becca had lost her dad to a glioblastoma brain tumor when she was only fourteen years old. He'd lived five years longer than the initial prognosis. She still teared up when she spoke about him. Hearing this from Garrett let me know that he was way ahead of me with Becca. Their bond was in a deeper place. I still had hometowns ahead of me, but I resigned myself to this new reality. I was toast.

I supposed I knew that already. I couldn't walk away, though. I had to go through the motions and let the rose petals drop where they may.

Nice Guys Finish Fourth

One night back in Virginia, before our unofficial moratorium on handicapping which one of us would walk off with Becca's heart, Jason, Garrett, and I thought we'd figured out who Becca was going to choose. At that moment, Leo was on his date with Becca, and I was pretty sure her final words to him would be *nice knowing you*. The guys agreed, all of us laughing nervously with the knowledge the same would eventually happen to some of us.

Discussions such as this one were fun; it was like talking about fantasy football. We turned over all the details, talked about the players, recapped each person's conversation with Becca, and analyzed every look, word, and gesture. Garrett asked what I thought would happen next, after Becca dumped Leo.

"I'm pretty sure it's going to break down like this: Blake is high up on her list, and I think it'll be him and the three of us in the hometowns."

Jason agreed with my assessment.

"I think you'll go fourth," I continued. "I'll go third, and I am thinking Blake will be the one."

Garrett wanted to know if I was sure about that, given that I was eliminating myself.

"Not one hundred percent," I said. "You're the wild card."

"And you think I'm going before you?" Jason asked.

"Only because they probably want my story for the fantasy suites," I replied. "They can play it up, like will he? Or won't he?"

It turned out I was mostly right. Garrett, Blake, Jason, and I were the four guys who made it to the hometowns. These were my best friends from the group, and I was happy for all of us. I knew Becca wasn't going to pick me in the end, so I was able to say goodbye to everyone in Nassau and mean it when I said, "Good luck." I flew back to LA with my producer, Robbie, who took over from Ruby as my full-time babysitter.

The two of us checked into a boutique hotel near West Hollywood, where we kept busy for the next four days while Becca went on her hometown dates with the other guys. We shopped, worked out, and visited my favorite steak house on the show's tab. I wondered how the other guys were doing—Garrett in Northern California, Jason in New York, and Blake in Bailey, Colorado.

Still prohibited from access to the Internet, I couldn't search for any spoilers about their hometowns. I could only hope mine went okay.

And it did, starting the moment Robbie and I landed in Denver and took our first breaths of cool Rocky Mountain air. I was excited to be there. To kick off the hometown, I led Becca around an outdoor farmers market. Truth be told, I'd never been there before. The producers had selected this trendy location. But Becca got a taste of the real me when we met with kids at the local children's hospital and I introduced her to the work I did with my Legacy Foundation. As I told her, these visits always made me a better person.

Confident of having made a strong, positive impression, I psyched myself up for the family dinner at my dad's house. I held my breath as Becca met my mom and dad, their respective spouses, my brother and his fiancée, Jennica, and my stepsiblings and aunts and uncles. Altogether, the group totaled eighteen. They weren't a family, they were a team. Team Colton. They were loving, protective, skeptical (*right, Mom?*), and totally, utterly unpredictable.

My dad, who'd spent the day preparing a dinner of Becca's and my favorites for dinner—salmon, potatoes, asparagus, and mac and cheese—was a straight shooter who was going to say whatever he wanted even with cameras pointed at him. My mom was even more of a wild card. She hated the show and hated me being on it even more, and she was more than willing to say so without any prompting.

I threw footballs. She threw f-bombs.

Love you, Mom!

When Becca and I got to the house, I knew it was going to be a make-or-break night for me. Actually, it was such a long night my dad's dinner went uneaten; if nothing else, it proved Becca and I had the stamina to go the distance. But other factors influenced her. My dad was blunt with Becca. He told her not to pick me if she wasn't sure, explaining, "It's better to have someone hurt now than down the road." My mom told Becca that she'd support us if we were ready, but I think she was playing to the camera and waiting until everyone cleared out so she could get me alone and ask, as she did, "Okay, what's next?"

Before she spoke with Becca, the two of us went off by ourselves and I told her that I was still a virgin. This was the first time I'd admitted it to her, and I was more nervous than when I'd told Becca. My producers gave me a ton of support leading up to the talk. They agreed it would be in my own best interests to tell my mom so she didn't find out on TV.

This kind of constant push for emotional honesty is what scared me the most about being on the show and also what I loved the most. It forced me to have meaningful conversations with my parents about topics that would have otherwise remained unspoken. In doing so, we got to know each other better and grew closer, especially my dad and me. I think he got to know me for more than just being a football player. We talked about real shit. We grew closer. And I'll take that any day.

It was two months of intensive relationship therapy, which I highly recommend. You don't have your cell phone. You aren't checking messages. There's no FOMO. You don't talk about bullshit. You focus on your relationship and trying to make it work, and for obvious reasons that touches every part of your entire life. Producers might suggest certain topics or issues, but they are like shrinks pushing you to confront things that you're uncomfortable with but that ultimately make you stronger, more self-aware, and truthful for having addressed them.

The hometowns finished, and before handing out her final rose, Becca flew back to LA and had a sit 'n' chat with her *Bachelor* BFFs Bekah Martinez, Kendall Long, Caroline Lunny, Seinne Fleming, and Tia. Of course Tia had to be there. I didn't see this part until it aired on TV, but Tia would tell Becca that she still had feelings for me and that would be the end of my relationship with Becca.

Obviously that set the stage for Tia and me meeting again on *Bachelor in Paradise,* except I wasn't thinking that far ahead. We still had the rose ceremony ahead of us.

We gathered at the mansion, our first time back in a while. Before the rose ceremony, I excused myself from the three other guys awaiting word of their fate and asked Chris Harrison to give me a download on the fantasy suites in case Becca extended an invitation to me. I thought it was a fun move given everything I'd revealed about myself on the show. What virgin wouldn't be curious about what went on in the fantasy suites? I wanted to know the basics, like what to pack and whether I should take a nap beforehand. Who better to give you "the talk" than Chris Harrison?

When Becca walked in to hand out the roses, she couldn't have looked more beautiful and in control. All of us guys were a little bit nervous and on edge as we waited to hear whether she would call our names. She had us in the palm of her hand, which I suppose is where we wanted to be. All of us had genuinely strong feelings for her, and none of us was ready to have them turned off. I assumed that my virginity made me a shoo-in for the fantasy suites. Who could possibly be more awkward, nervous, and funny in that situation than me?

But soon it was painfully apparent that Becca's thoughts differed from mine. I didn't get a rose. I was surprised and hurt. Not crushed. Not heartbroken. Not pretending to be okay when I wasn't. Not stopped in my tracks and wondering where I went wrong or what mistakes I might have made. I was just hurt in the sense that I had been honest about myself and opened my heart and believed the emotions I felt were reciprocated, but in the end it wasn't enough, and it wasn't me. It was that kind of hurt.

It if looked worse, it was the suddenness and the shock of it actually happening and realizing this dream ride was over. I said goodbye to Jason, Garrett, and Blake, and then Becca and I parted ways by wishing each other the best. There were no hard feelings. Both of us understood the reasons even if they weren't fully articulated. We went through something together. We would remain friends.

My producer Robbie stopped me as I walked to the car waiting to take me back to the hotel. He gave me a hug and asked how I was doing.

"Are you sure you're all right?" Robbie asked.

"Yeah, I'm good," I said. "I mean, it sort of sucks and it sort of doesn't."

He rode with me back to the hotel. I stayed there for the next two days and caught up on sleep and my workouts. It felt good to be off schedule and do nothing but decompress from nearly three months of being inside *The Bachelorette* bubble. When Robbie returned my cell phone to me, it was like he handed me back the keys to my real life, though, as he knew and I would discover, nothing about my life would be the same again. "Congratulations," he said. "You're going to be famous. People are going to know who you are."

I laughed and told him that I was flying back to Denver in the morning.

"We'll still be in touch," he said. "We'll talk throughout the show and stuff."

"Cool."

"And who knows what's next. You'd be a good bachelor."

I hadn't given much if any thought to that, but I sure liked the sound of it now.

"Really?"

"It's possible," he said.

PART THREE

*The World's Most
Famous Virgin*

Paradise

The next day I powered up my phone. I had 1,600 text messages, 240 missed calls, and over 10,000 emails. Going through all of them was impossible. Never mind responding. I phoned my parents with an update, and my dad said, "Dang, I guess we blew it for you." Although Becca later indicated their talk had influenced her, at least in part, I assured him that she was never going to pick me and gave him the full download of the experience a couple of days later when I got back to Denver.

Despite what she'd told Becca, my mom was relieved I didn't return with a future daughter-in-law. We debated the difference of meeting a girl in a bar, a dating app, or on a reality TV show and in the end agreed it came down to chemistry, timing, desire, compatibility, trust, and whatever the hell it was that Cupid put on the tip of his arrow.

"It either happens or it doesn't," my mom said.

"It didn't happen for me," I said.

"Don't get me started again," she said, laughing.

It was my pleasure not to. Happy to be back in Denver, I slept in, worked out, and went on hikes with my dog, Sniper. Talk about unconditional love. He was thirteen years old, ancient in dog years, and I could see age taking its toll on him. I didn't want to think about having to one day find another companion—at least the four-legged kind. Finding a two-legged human companion, though, was very much top of mind.

During those first few days back in Denver, I engaged in a back-and-forth with producers about *Bachelor in Paradise*. Before I left Los Angeles, they pitched me the idea of going on the highly rated summer-oriented show. Shooting began in two weeks. I had less than a week to decide. But I didn't need that much time. *Paradise* didn't look that way to me. I didn't see the fun. Thinking about hanging out on the beach, partying, and talking trash about other people made me anxious. It wasn't me.

The producers listened to my reservations and said they understood. But they really wanted me to do it and argued I needed to complete my story—for the fans and the franchise.

"What do you mean?" I asked. "My story is done. Becca dumped me."

"No, people want to know what's up with you and Tia."

Got it. This was television, and I was now a character in their reality drama. No one made any promises, but I got the feeling that if *Paradise* went well I might have a good shot at becoming the Bachelor. The show's selection process was well-documented online and in the press, but it was also based on common sense. They looked at fan favorites. They factored in desirability—like are women into him. They also wanted to make sure the Bachelor wanted to and was ready to fall in love and get married. Authenticity was crucial. And then there was the X factor. Did it feel right?

I had my own X factor. This was my life, my real life, and before making any decision, I had to ask myself some questions: Did I want to be the Bachelor? And if so, how badly? Badly enough to go to *Paradise,* as Tia had foreshadowed all those months ago? Badly enough to engage with Tia again? It wasn't as if we had a real relationship. We didn't leave a romance broken or unresolved. We'd spent a weekend together and developed a friendship built on text messages.

But that no longer mattered. As our story evolved, Bachelor fans turned it into something else. They liked the drama of Tia returning to the show, confiding her feelings for me to Becca, and wanting to explore whether there was any chance of it developing into a relationship. It was a good story and one a lot of people would relate to.

I called around and learned more about *Paradise*. They took a group of popular guys and girls from past seasons of *The Bachelorette* and *The Bachelor*, sprinkled in a few wild cards, and put everyone up at a remote beach resort in Mexico. It was a dating-themed *Lord of the Flies*. Worse, the conditions were kind of rough: There was no air-conditioning, the huts didn't have any doors, and bugs were everywhere. It was all the things I hate—insects, humidity, dirt, lack of privacy. Sort of like *Survivor* after all!

But I wanted to be the Bachelor. From the first time I heard the idea mentioned, I thought about myself in that role. I didn't know how much I wanted it, though, until I faced the possibility of not being the Bachelor. I wasn't done with the excitement or the people involved in creating it. I also wasn't done with the experience itself. I had this sixth sense–like feeling that it was going to work for me. If I was the Bachelor, it would be me and thirty beautiful, bright women eager to win my affection. I liked those odds.

I was going to find love if I didn't give up.

Which meant saying yes to *Paradise* was in my best interests.

I called the producers. I was in.

I reached out to Ben Higgins, who'd appeared on *The Bachelorette* before starring in season twenty of *The Bachelor*. He supported my decision. You want to pick your battles, he said, adding that it was too early for me to even have any battles. He encouraged me to be a team player.

"*Paradise* is what you make of it," he said. "If you want to party, you can party. If you want to chill, you can chill."

Good advice.

Exactly what I needed to hear.

As I finalized details with the show, I thought about Tia. She'd tried to reach me while I was away shooting *The Bachelorette* and I still hadn't responded to her. But she was top of mind for obvious reasons I had to figure out. Why couldn't I figure them out? She possessed all the qualities that made someone attractive. There was the obvious, and there was the part of Tia that shined even brighter when you got to know her.

Why then didn't I feel that spark? That special chemistry that drew people to each other? I just didn't. And for that reason I didn't see us together.

Then again, I felt like I owed it to Tia to see if she was right and if maybe I missed something as a result of being so focused on Becca.

If she liked me that much . . .

But what if I was right? What if we got to Mexico and it was a disaster? Or what if one of us clicked with someone else there?

This show! It could drive you crazy!

The best I could do was resolve to not mislead her. I would tell her that I wanted to keep my options open. It might be her. It might be someone else. Or no one else.

With that settled, I got ready to leave for Mexico. I packed half the amount of recommended clothing as a way of reminding myself that I intended to be there two weeks or less. If I stayed longer, *Paradise* would have a potential crossover episode with *Dating Naked*. On my way to the airport, I stopped at Home Depot and bought a portable swamp cooler for my hotel room there, which proved a smart move.

The hotel where the show initially put me up was fabulous but boring. I binge-watched Harry Potter movies and ate so much guacamole and nachos that when I did finally step onto the *Paradise* beach, it was with the thud of an overstuffed piñata.

Chris Harrison welcomed me with a date card. On my own after that, I wandered in as my former *Bachlorette* compadre Chris Randone was talking to some of the guys about having dated Tia the previous night. I was happy for her—and them. As I told Chris, I was there to explore the many options available to me. It might be Tia. It might be someone else.

My date card enabled me to choose anyone I wanted for a one-on-one. I spent time with Kendall Long, came close to asking out Bibiana Julian, and eventually decided I wanted to use my card to date Angela Amezcua, a model from South Carolina who'd been on Nick Viall's season of *The Bachelor*. She seemed fun, athletic, outgoing, and not the person everyone thought I'd go for, and the naughty boy in me wanted to do something unexpected. Nothing wrong with shaking things up, right?

Except I knew the reason I was there—and so did everyone else. I heard the girls whispering on the beach when I didn't go for Tia right away. Then I did the expected and asked her on a date. The two of us spent the day lounging on a yacht. Comfortable together, we laughed, talked, and melted into the sun-drenched comfort of the moment. I was clear about not wanting to commit to anything, but Tia wasn't looking for a commitment as much as she was a new beginning, and when she asked, "Do you want to try again?" I leaned in and kissed her.

I'd realized sometime midseason on *The Bachelorette*: when in doubt, kiss. It was easier than trying to think about what to say and much more fun.

For the second part of our date, Tia and I climbed on Jet Skis and sped across the water. It was a perfect metaphor for the two of us. We had fun without really going anywhere. At the rose ceremony, Tia gave hers to Chris and it looked like I was done. I'm sure this was punishment for my refusal to plunge into a relationship with her; I continued to insist that I wanted to keep all my options open. Was it possible to dash her hopes and remain a good guy to fans?

In what I took as a positive sign, Bibiana offered me her rose and kept me in the mix. Far from being over, my story continued to build. Becca dropped in for a girl-to-girl pep talk with Tia and to set the record straight with me. She assured me that Tia was not the reason she sent me home. She had been in love with Garrett for a long time, she said, and everything else had been about exploring her options and making sure he was the one.

She told me not to rule out Tia. She insisted that Tia's feelings for me were real and urged me to give it a try with her.

Tia sent me the same signals. I'd wanted to keep my options open. She was an option. What the hell, right?

I got a moment alone with Tia and made it count.

"Let's just really see if it's us," I told her. "No games. Let's see if we can do this and go from here."

She agreed. And we tried.

But here's what no one knew until it came gushing out of me in a boatload of tears. From the moment I finished speaking with Becca, I was an emotional wreck. I know people saw something else on the outside. Inside, I was a mess. Talking to Becca had reminded me of the emotions I'd experienced with her and the importance of being honest with myself and sharing that with Tia. Even as Tia and I strolled the beach and danced together in town, I knew I was pretending things were okay, and they weren't. I felt dishonest, vulnerable, and all too human.

When I handed Tia a rose on Guy's Night, I crossed the personal line I'd set for myself on *Paradise*. I could hear myself saying, "Don't lie." And what was I doing? That was my bad. That wasn't me. I didn't want to lead Tia on or lie to her. I also didn't want to be anyone other than who I really was—honest, imperfect, and not in love with Tia. The next day I broke up with her, and in the midst of all the explaining I did to try to make sure she understood and didn't get too upset, I felt like shit.

On the flight home I purchased the in-flight Wi-Fi and texted Tia. She assured me that she was okay. She'd said goodbye to her pals on the beach and, like me, had gotten a chance to take a breath and get some perspective as she left the bubble that was *Paradise* and headed home. I felt terrible about breaking up with her, but I also knew it was the right thing to do, and she agreed. We were better off as friends, and we've remained friends. To this day, she is one of my most trusted confidantes.

Back in Denver, I slept for eighteen hours straight and went to the gym. Even though I'd only been gone a couple of weeks, my body was out of whack and my head was only a little better. I was off. I needed the long sleep and a hard workout to reset my life. I wanted to get back to normal. But my life hadn't been normal since I left football. Consider my Google calendar since then: Shoulder surgery. A relationship with Aly. *The Bachelorette. Bachelor in Paradise.* I was freestylin' my life. Was normal even possible? Did it matter? At the moment, I just wanted to feel good and figure out WTF was going on.

I checked in with Jason, Blake, and Garrett, and the three of us caught up. Talking to them helped me process the past couple of weeks with Tia. I spoke with my dad, too, and warned him that I cried on *Paradise*.

"How bad?" he asked.

"Pretty bad," I said.

My poor dad. Over the years, he'd caught me questioning my sexual identity, going public on reality TV as a twenty-six-year-old virgin, and now I was preparing him to see me bawling my eyes out on TV while having some kind of emotional breakdown.

"Dad, am I the all-American linebacker you expected?"

"You're even better," he said. "Nothing surprises me anymore."

He might have spoken too soon.

The World's Most Famous Virgin

I needed a couple of weeks before I felt comfortable back in my own home. I'd barely lived there since renting it days before I left for *The Bachelorette*. Now, about four months later, every day was an adventure in discovering where I'd put the few things I owned, like dishes, blankets, and old football jerseys. The place didn't reflect a lifestyle as much as it did a life in search of a style. I relied on the dozens of little soaps and shampoos I'd taken from hotels and snacks I'd saved from planes and photo shoots. This was no way to live, and yet somehow . . . well, I remember one day, as I walked around eating a meal I'd had delivered, I had this feeling of not being able to find my life. Where had I put it?

To find out, all I had to do was watch TV. Season fourteen of *The Bachelorette* was scheduled to premiere on May 28, 2018. With a week to go, I was counting down the days. I remembered the fateful words my producer Robbie said after Becca sent me home: "Congratulations, you're now famous." Having grown up in the era of reality TV, not to mention schooling myself in dozens of seasons of *The Bachelorette* and *The Bachelor*, I knew what he meant. What I didn't—and couldn't—know was how that would affect me. I was excited and scared.

Very scared. On the show, I'd opened up about personal issues in ways I'd never shared with my family or close friends, and it was all about to get served up on TV to ten million viewers and opened up for discussion to even more people inside the Twitterverse. It was every OMG and WTF moment I'd ever had wrapped into one. I prepared my mom and dad before I started to trend. When they asked if I was ready, I laughed nervously and said I honestly didn't know what to expect.

On the plus side, I figured time was on my side. My date with Becca wherein I talked to her about my virginity didn't happen until week seven. All the Tia drama in the earlier episodes would be an easy warmup, like a stretching exercise, before I opened up to Becca about love and loss and . . . uh, that other thing. I could manage.

Relieved, I helped plan a viewing party at my dad's house for the season premiere. My dad invited a bunch of his friends and put out a buffet. My mom brought her crew and arrived with more food. A party-time atmosphere filled the packed house, and I had much more fun than I thought—until the show began to wrap up.

That's when the bomb was dropped. Chris Harrison introduced a super tease of the rest of the season and suddenly everyone heard my voice, shaky and emotional: "I've been hiding something from her." Then they cut to my dinner date with Becca in the Bahamas. First an establishing shot. Then a close-up. My face filled the screen. "I was ashamed . . . and I made up lies . . . because, um, I still am, I am a virgin. . . ."

Arrgggghhhhh!

If it had been possible to unscrew my head and toss it out the window, I would've done so at that moment to avoid the way everyone in the house was looking at me. I happened to be in the middle of the room. There was no getting up and sneaking out. This was that moment where I knew my life was going to change. Whether it was for better or worse, I had no idea. All I knew was that it was going to be a little—okay, maybe a lot—embarrassing, and I had to get through it.

I put my head down, shut my eyes, and took a deep breath. It was as if time stopped momentarily, and when it started again, I was looking around at everyone with a self-conscious, good-natured, shit-happens smile.

"Well, that was a little tough," I said.

I turned toward my dad. He was shaking his head in disbelief but also smiling at me.

"Do you have anything else you want to tell us?" he said.

Everyone laughed.

"I don't know." I scratched my hair. "Let me think. It's hard to download everything I said over three months of my life."

"We don't need *everything*," he joked.

I knew that moment, however uncomfortable it made me, was a necessary step in owning who I was and figuring out who I was going to be. Everyone has one of those types of moments—maybe more than one. I don't think they're supposed to be easy. But self-truth and honesty had to begin with me. It was like lifting weights. Can I bench 250 pounds? Yes. Prove it. Then, okay, I lifted that much, can I do more? Yes—and let's see how much more. Over the years I'd lied to my teammates, some of my coaches, and my friends. I had told them I'd hooked up with girls when I had actually spent the night in my bedroom watching *Friends*. It had been easier to lie than tell the truth. Except over time the lie required more lies. Until I found myself in this social experiment called *The Bachelorette*.

There, the lies stopped. They had to. If I was going to discover my full potential, if I was going to have a chance at falling in love, if I was going to be able to answer the question, how will I know, then I had to not only tell the truth, I had to live it. If I was going to be honest with someone else, I had to first be honest with myself.

And, as everyone had just seen, I was doing exactly that. I took the things that had crushed me in high school and embarrassed me in college and put them out there for the whole world to see and discuss. In some weird, unplanned, therapeutic, and self-actualized way, I was actually stronger for it—or becoming stronger.

For the next twenty-four hours, my phone blew up. My social media blew up, too. My Twitter went nuts. Overnight, I went from thirty thousand followers to nearly two hundred thousand. The DMs from family, friends, former teammates, and tons of strangers were very supportive. "Good for you." "I have respect for you." "You'll know when the time is right." One of my high school football coaches shared that he and his wife had both waited until they were married. All of them underscored how important it is to be yourself.

After the premiere, I watched subsequent episodes at home by myself or at my dad's with whoever was there on Monday night, and of course I texted with Jason, Blake, and a few others as the show aired and in the days afterward. It was always fun to process the reaction. I was pleased with the way I came off in Las Vegas when I opened up to Becca about why my first relationship had ended. I was able to see the effect my honesty had on her.

It was two weeks later when my dinner date with Becca in the Bahamas finally aired that I finally understood my life was going to be different. Within the span of a few hours, I was the world's most famous virgin. When that episode aired, I was in the Dominican Republic at my brother's wedding, and I remember being more anxious than I'd ever been in my life. I couldn't watch or keep up on social media. Every news outlet had my virginity in their headlines. In a thoughtful gesture, Becca sent a message saying she was proud of me for opening up the way I did, with such feeling and honesty, and she hoped I was well.

Was I well? I had no idea. I was shell-shocked is what I was.

But hearing from Becca went a long way in calming me down. She took some flak for the way it appeared she got up from the table as if she were torn between keeping me or not. As I mentioned earlier though, she was sensitive and perfectly respectful and in no way torn by my candor. The rest of the world—at least those who cared—felt the same way. The messages that reached me were positive and supportive, though I also saw the comments from those who said I wasn't cut out to be in a relationship because I hadn't had sex or what they called enough relationship experience.

I wasn't about to tell people how to think. But no amount of experience makes you more suitable for a relationship. Love is love. It's either there or it's not. You don't get better at falling in love or making it last, not in the way you can improve at communicating or learning to be more patient or listening to a different point of view. The only thing you can do is recognize it and then treat it like the most precious thing in your life.

I watched my last episode, the hometowns, from the Denver Children's Hospital, where I organized a viewing party for patients and staff, including some of the kids featured in Becca's and my visit there. We hung out, ate cupcakes, and played games. They laughed and cheered when they saw themselves, and some of them hugged me and told me not to be sad when I was sent home, as if I were the one who needed the TLC.

It kept everything in perspective.

Holding Pattern

With *The Bachelorette* and *Paradise* behind me, I found myself back where I was before my audition, when I knew I was done with football and unsure about what to do next. There was one difference that was now part of my daily life and impossible to ignore. I had hundreds of thousands of people following me on social media.

Anonymous no more, I put off job hunting until *Bachelorette* and *Paradise* were off the air to avoid dealing with people in the workforce watching me every Monday night. An even more important reason for putting the job search on hold was *The Bachelor*. I was in regular contact with producers about becoming the next Bachelor, as were several other guys, but the announcement wouldn't be made until the end of August.

The show was a three-month commitment, and then who knew what would happen. I couldn't get a job and then ask for half the year off if I was tapped for season twenty-three. Most places had maternity and paternity leaves, mental-health leaves, and so on. None had leave to be the Bachelor. It put my life in a holding pattern until they reached a decision.

I worked out every day, but that wasn't enough. My dad, seeing that I was struggling without any structure to my day, had me come into his State Farm office and answer phones and learn the business. I also took online courses and started down the road to getting certified as a mortgage broker. I missed working toward the goals football had always provided: improving skills, prepping for games, working toward a win.

By midsummer, my communication with the show about *The Bachelor* grew more frequent and detailed. I learned it was between me, Jason, and Blake. Producers were monitoring our popularity as the season progressed. At the end of July, I returned to LA to tape "The Men Tell All" episode for *The Bachelorette*. I didn't know what formula producers measured popularity by, but I wanted to use the platform to grow mine. I had to find a way within the hour-long show to create some positive buzz.

I traded a couple of one-liners with Jordan, which played well. Earlier in the season, we'd had some minor differences, but we'd moved past those long ago and I was certain that fans saw we were having fun with each other. As I looked around, only one guy had gotten under my skin the entire season: Jean Blanc, a smart dude from Boston who was getting his masters from Duke. He was a schemer who'd made legit enemies among the guys in Utah when he'd told Becca that he loved her, then took it back seconds later.

It was extremely uncool, and when that incident came up on "The Men Tell All," I decided to tell him how I felt. It seemed like something fans and some of the other guys seated around me would support. You can't lose defending a beautiful woman's honor.

"You played every one of us," I said. "You lied to every one of us. And you lied to Becca."

Jean Blanc was pissed.

"Chris, I'm not going to talk to little boys right now," he said.

"It's okay, he'll take it back in three seconds," I quipped.

That got a laugh. It also got Jean Blanc angrier.

"Colton, you're acting like a pussy," he said. "But you've never been fucked. So I don't know what's going on."

His shot was a cheap one that only reminded those in Bachelor Nation that I was the good guy in this exchange. As far as I was concerned, mission accomplished. He went on TMZ claiming I owed him an apology. But I was done with him, and the show's producers concurred. I remember someone said, "What's that thing our mothers told us about sticks and stones? Just ignore him. He'll go away."

A few weeks later, Becca presented her final rose to Garrett and then *Bachelor in Paradise* began spicing up summer's primetime lineup. *Paradise* may not have lived up to its name for me, but once it began to air, I enjoyed the positive reaction it generated for me. They were interested in this next chapter between Tia and me, and when it turned out to be the last one, they understood the relationship couldn't be forced. I even got props for trying.

Right after the show ended, though, my phone rang. It was my dad.

"Holy shit, Colt," he said. "You told me you cried, but that was more than a cry."

By then I had flown to LA several times to meet with producers in person about *The Bachelor*. I sensed that I was in the final lap or two. I didn't know, of course, but I'd filled out more questionnaires and spoken at length with some of the show's senior producers. I felt good about the meetings. We had a good rapport. They knew me well and seemed to like me. The energy was good. I was reminded of the way I felt when I went through the process for *The Bachelorette*. Excited, open, hopeful. One important difference? My virginity was no longer a secret. Nor had I lost it. Which seemed like a good thing. I was asked if I was willing to experience a first time were I to meet the right person on the show.

Absolutely, I said, without hesitation. For me, the only issue was finding the right person. Not coincidentally, that was the reason I wanted to be the Bachelor. Forget all the perks and notoriety, my intention was genuine and unchanged from when I filled out the application to be on *The Bachelorette*. I really did want to fall in love and get married. I really did need help finding the right person. I really did trust the show to do a better job that I could do on my own. And if all that happened, I really did want to go all the way.

Absolutely, I said, adding that the issue was finding the right person, which was the number one reason I was into being the Bachelor. It was true. All the perks and notoriety aside, my motives were genuine and the same as when I applied to be on *The Bachelorette*. I really did want to fall in love and get married; and I really did need help finding the right person; and if all that happened, I really did want to go all the way.

I sensed the producers appreciated what they heard and liked me as much as I liked them. As I've said many times, they knew me inside and out—probably better than I knew myself. I said I'd do everything I could to ensure a great show, and they knew what I meant was that if given the shot, I'd lead with my heart and trust the rest would follow.

I must've said something right. My next meeting was with *The Bachelor*'s chief executive, show creator Mike Fleiss, a brash, smart, creative guy and natural provocateur. The doors to his office were massive, maybe fourteen feet tall, made of thick wood, and gave the impression of going in to meet the king. Inside, the king was waiting for me. He wore a black T-shirt and jeans. A fan of my former football team, the San Diego Chargers, he greeted me by saying his buddy, Chargers GM Tom Telesco, had told him that I'd left them.

"Yeah, sort of," I said, not wanting to disagree with the boss, yet knowing the answer was a bit more complicated than the version he knew. "I got hurt. Tore my hamstring. They offered to keep me on the practice squad, but I thought they'd cut my ass the next day. I chose to go on the injured reserve list, which credited me with three games and qualified me for the NFL pension. It was a smart business decision, I think."

One question that came up: Was I willing to lose my virginity?

"If I meet the right person and fall in love," I said.

I left the meeting confident it had gone well. I knew Jason and Blake were going through the same interview process. We were open with each other. We shared details of our interviews, our meetings, and contracts in a group text that included one of the producers, who knew we were buddies. None of us knew who might be leading the pack.

But I was confident that I had one thing in my favor that the other guys didn't, and I knew they could never in this lifetime get it: I was the world's most famous virgin—and giving me another chance to address that status in the fantasy suites would be must-see TV.

Good Morning America

As the decision-making ticked into its final seconds, I kept thinking of reasons for producers to pick me. Obsessed, I thought my lack of experience might prove to be an advantage over the other guys. Even if their background checks were spotless, which they were, I was still the safest bet among us in this era of #MeToo sensitivities. Other than one well-publicized romance, I'd spent most of my adolescence and early adulthood in my room, watching reruns of *Friends*.

I remembered something else. Before taping the *Paradise* reunion special, I'd been fitted for two suits. Producers never explained why I was being measured instead of being instructed to wear my own suit. And why two suits? Was this a sign? Maybe for an appearance on *Good Morning America* to announce the next Bachelor?

Finally, before I began white-boarding March Madness–like brackets, the wait was over. It was Monday morning, September 3, and I was playing in a full-court basketball game, as I did three mornings each week. It was a pickup game with a bunch of older guys who hustled up and down the court. They were there for cardio, not to drop buckets, which was the reason I liked this particular game. Midway through our game, my Apple watch pinged.

In full stride when I heard it, I looked down and saw it was an email from one of show's producers addressed to me, Jason, and Blake. I stopped to read the full message. "Hey, I'll have some news for you early this week," it said.

Early this week turned out to be moments later. The same producer who'd sent the email called. I let it go straight to message. I had a feeling I was going to be disappointed and decided to call him back later. Then I received a text. "Call me when you can." The dude really wanted to talk to me. When I looked up, the ball was coming straight at me. I blocked it with my palm, dribbled twice, and dropped a 17-footer from the right of the key to put my team ahead and win the game.

Normally the winning team stays on the court, but I grabbed my towel, took a swig from my water bottle, and said, "Hey guys, give me a minute. I gotta call somebody." I never returned to the game. I called the producer back and the first words he uttered, even before hello, were, "Congratulations! Do you want to be the Bachelor?"

He had to get a yes from me before he could break the news to Jason and Blake.

"Can't wait," I said. "Let's do it."

There wasn't much advance warning. They wanted to make the announcement the next day on ABC's *Good Morning America*. He said they'd get me on a flight to New York later that afternoon. It was like going from 0 to 150 mph in six seconds; I nearly suffered whiplash. I went from a guy with nothing to do to someone who would soon be the subject of intense debate and disappointment (for fans of Jason and Blake) and celebration throughout Bachelor Nation and across social media.

Breathless, excited, speed-dialing my parents, I went home to pack. Within the hour, I received congratulatory texts from Jason and Blake. Producers called with additional details, including a stern warning: no pictures with fans in either the Denver or New York airports. They'd turn into spoilers. Bloggers would take the photos as an unofficial confirmation before the official announcement.

I swore my family to secrecy for the next twenty-four hours. Only my mom expressed skepticism. She didn't understand why I wanted to go on the show for the third time.

"I just think it's really messed up," she said.

"Maybe I'll fall in love," I countered.

"Sure—and maybe I'll be the next Oprah," she said.

I laughed all the way to the first-class lounge at the airport. It was an upgrade from coach travel for *The Bachelorette*. At JFK International Airport in New York, I was met by Nancy Pool, who would be my lead producer throughout the season. She whisked me into a waiting car and spent most of the next hour asking how I felt and letting me know what was in store for me for the next twenty-four hours.

My mind was a blur as I checked into a suite at a midtown hotel near *GMA*'s studio in Times Square. I should've gone to sleep, but I had too much adrenaline to shut my eyes, so I checked my phone and found a text from Tia. Somehow she'd found out I was going to be the next Bachelor. Outside of my family, only Jason and Blake knew. But this inner world of the Bachelor had its own crazy pipeline for news and gossip. It was no different from sports, politics, or Hollywood.

"Did you know you were going to be the Bachelor while we were together?" Tia asked.

"I just found out seven hours ago," I said.

"You didn't know before?"

"Only that it was always a possibility," I said. "You knew that, too."

This was like high school, but after a long, late-night debrief, Tia said she wanted me to have a good time. She wished me luck.

The morning came fast and started with a slight panic when

the suit I had been fitted for a few weeks earlier in LA didn't arrive. Fortunately, I brought my own, more casual backup and wore that to the *GMA* studio. While in the makeup chair, I sipped my second coffee of the morning and before I knew it I was answering questions opposite *GMA* host Michael Strahan, one of my football heroes when I was in high school. It was a lot to take in.

The reaction from Bachelor Nation was mixed, as I expected. Fans of both Jason and Blake made their disappointment known. "Nooo!" posted one person. "Not him," another said. "So disappointed." Some of the journalists and bloggers who covered the show were more blatant in their disapproval, like *Entertainment Weekly*'s resident expert Kristen Baldwin, who declared I was the "totally wrong choice to be the Bachelor." I thought her take was a little silly; she pushed for Wills Reid out of appreciation for his fashion sense and dissed me for liking dogs. How do you criticize someone for *liking dogs*?

I checked social media every spare minute I had. The passionate responses served as a reminder of the central fact of *The Bachelor*: It was about the fans. They had their favorites. They were passionate and loyal. They paid attention to everything. And they were committed. I did feel they would get behind me once the season began. Whether or not I was their number one, they knew me as a guy who was true to myself, who didn't lie, and who was going to hand out roses for the right reasons.

In most ways, I was like them. I believed in romance and love, and I wanted my season to end with a proposal and a happily ever after.

After the appearance on *GMA* and interviews with dozens of other media outlets, my phone filled up with calls and texts from family, friends, and former classmates and teammates offering congratulations and encouragement. Jason and Blake sent awesome messages again. Becca wished me well and offered friendly advice on little things, like making sure I had a jar of peanut butter nearby for long days that would make me hangry. "And be good. Keep your mouth shut," she joked.

I think the last thing I did before life was irrevocably altered was text my old producers, Ruby and Robbie. I knew they'd be working with the girls. "Stay with the good ones," I messaged. "I'm going to be trusting you."

Neither of them responded. I didn't think they would and I didn't care.

I was ready.

This was going to be fun.

Stylin'

With only two and a half weeks until my first rose ceremony, I went to work in my new role as soon as I was back in Denver. When I woke up that first morning, I saw a video crew waiting for me. My introductory video package was an extensive production. After following me for a day in Denver, we all traveled to Minneapolis, where my Legacy Foundation presented an AffloVest to our sixth recipient before a Vikings–49ers game. The smile on the little guy who got it was a great start.

Then they shot me regrouping with a few former Charger teammates before a game in San Diego. It was my idea, and in theory, a fun one. During warm-ups, I went on the field and talked with linebackers Kyle Emanuel and Nick Dzubnar. We were interrupted by Denzel Perryman, another buddy from the defense, who ran over, barged into the scene, and shared his enthusiasm for my new role.

"So you got thirty of them *thangs* and you get to choose one of them?" he said.

I nodded nervously, aware this was a little raw for ABC.

"Yeah, I get thirty women," I said.

"You lucky son of a bitch," he replied, slapping me on the back.

I was taking heat for being described in the media as a former NFL star. This had happened with *The Bachelorette*, too, but the press was more intense this time. The problem was in the characterization of me as a star. I couldn't help the language journalists and bloggers used when they wrote about me. For the record, though, I never called myself a star or said anything other than what I knew was true: I played on the practice squads for three teams. But that made me an NFL player, an accomplishment I will be proud of forever—and I have the scars on my shoulder to prove it.

I made one final trip back to Denver to say my goodbyes to my family and my beloved dog, Sniper, and went to sleep early. I was supposed to get on a flight the next morning at 6:30 a.m. My car service pickup was at 4:30 a.m. In the thrall of all the excitement, I apparently didn't set my alarm correctly and missed both the car service and the plane. My eyes didn't open until six thirty, but then I moved like lightning. I sped to the airport, booked another flight while I was driving, parked my car, texted my dad that he'd have to pick it up, and finally I texted my producer that I was going to be late.

I didn't admit that I'd missed my flight—the first and only flight I've ever missed. I figured things could only get better from here.

They did. The next day I showed up at Cary Fetman's house for the first of three straight ten-hour days of wardrobe fittings. As the show's chief wardrobe stylist, Cary had one of the most particular, important, and exclusive jobs on the show. He styled Chris Harrison and the Bachelor or Bachelorette, depending on which show was in production. No one else benefitted from his immaculate taste.

We had met before, briefly, when he helped me pick out two suits for the *Paradise* reunion show, including the so-called backup suit that never made it to New York for *GMA*. I suspected that fitting might have been a ploy to get my measurements, but I forgot to ask. Once Cary said hello, my head was totally focused on the here and now.

"I was hoping it would be you," he said. "You were just so nice and professional, and I appreciated that."

Cary had a best friend–like quality that made him immediately likable. He smiled broadly as he showed me around his place. My eyes went first to a table filled with an array of fresh salads, breads, and fruits, along with juice and coffee, enough to feed the two of us plus the thirty contestants were they to suddenly materialize in desperate want of a healthy California meal. Then I noticed racks and racks of clothes in his living room. It looked like the entire men's department at Bloomingdale's had been crammed into this one room.

"How the hell are you living here right now?" I said.

Cary shook his head.

"This isn't the half of it," he said.

He took me down to his basement and turned on the light to reveal more racks of clothes.

"We haven't even brought these up yet," he said.

We went back upstairs and talked before going through any of the clothes. Cary already had a vision for me that mixed seasonal, casual, and sophisticated suits. He liked cool prints and was big on spiffing up a T-shirt and jeans with a sport coat or lightweight leather jacket. When he asked for my thoughts, I gestured toward all the clothes and just said, "Holy shit, this looks like the good life already."

And it was. Dolce & Gabbana, Prada, Gucci. His doorbell rang at least four times, with more packages being dropped off. When I thought there couldn't possibly be any more, Cary put his laptop in front of me and said, "Here, order whatever shoes you need." I already had hookups at a few places, I told him. I could get shoes for free. "Nah, just order from here. Whatever you think you're going to need."

He had me pick out all my rose ceremony suits and rank them from what I wanted on night one to what I would want for the finale. We discussed which ones gave me options to wear a tie or go without one. I rounded out the collection with button-downs, tees, jeans, Henleys—my favorite—and a few pairs of boots.

I can't emphasize how indulgent it felt to be spoiled like this, especially by someone as talented as Cary. I'd brought my own clothes on *The Bachelorette* and *Bachelor in Paradise*. Now I was being given a wardrobe teeming with designer labels that would fill eleven suitcases. It was quite a turnaround—and Cary wasn't finished. He brought out a rack of bathing suits and told me to pick as many as I wanted.

"That's a lot of bathing suits," I said.

He confirmed the obvious with a friendly nod, after which I looked at Eileen Hannigan, a coordinating producer who was keeping an eye on me. She worked with Nancy and ran a lot of the logistics. I flashed her a naughty smile and then looked back at Cary.

"This must mean I'm going someplace warm," I said to Cary.

He shrugged without making a sound.

Fine, I didn't have to know everything right away. Two days later, as I walked through my hotel lobby after breakfast, I was intercepted by my producer. Smiling, Nancy said it was time. She asked for my cell phone. I checked for any last-minute texts and looked over my social media one last time before relinquishing my phone for the next three months. I was officially cut off from the outside world. Soon it would be like that for thirty single women looking forward to meeting me. We'd create our own reality.

I couldn't wait.

Ellen

Like everyone, I have my issues. I can be anxious and controlling. I worry and stress about what I'm doing with my life, or not doing with it, as happened while I waited to hear whether I was going to be the Bachelor. But when producers handed me the keys to an old orange Bronco and told me to drive around Malibu while they shot B-roll for my video package, I had no doubt that I was in the exact right place in the world doing exactly what I was supposed to be doing.

I drove through Malibu Canyon and along the coast. I admired the surfers and the crashing waves. The wind blew in my face. Every song on the radio sounded like it had been written for that moment. The only thing missing was someone to sit in the passenger seat, and that was why I was there—to find that person.

I drove to the hotel that would be my new home and parked in front. The crew pulled up behind me. As I walked across the parking lot, with the truck's keys dangling from my finger, I couldn't stop smiling. Inside the hotel, Nancy led me to a suite at the back of the first floor, my room. The hotel had taken over two other adjacent rooms—one for my wardrobe, which Cary and his team had already filled with racks of clothes; and the second was refurbished as an on-camera production studio for instant, in-the-moment interviews.

My room was the largest of the three. A treadmill had been placed in the living room, as I'd requested, so I could get my miles in anytime I wanted.

"This place is sick," I said.

I went to sleep that night trying to imagine the girls who'd be joining me on the show. As I knew from past experience, their pictures had been posted online. They were available for everyone to see, except me. Without access to the Internet, I had to rely on my imagination, and it was running wild with possibilities as I wondered what the girls would look like, where they'd be from, and whether I'd click with any of them.

Would I find a best friend?

What would her name be? What would make her laugh? What music would she like? Would she be tall or short? Athletic?

So many questions.

In the morning, producers used their set of keys to enter my room and make sure I was awake, which I was, sort of. I said a groggy good morning and pulled the sheets over me, reminding them that I slept in the buff. If they were going to enter without knocking, I warned it was at their own risk.

Once coiffed and outfitted in dark jeans, a button-down, and a blazer, I tackled my first official responsibility as the Bachelor, an appearance on *Ellen*, the award-winning daytime talk show. I was excited to meet Ellen DeGeneres. I watched her show in college when I couldn't fall asleep and became a major fan. My roommates gave me a lot of shit about that, too. They'd talk about what'd happened at the bar the night before and I'd tell them about the way Ellen had given some deserving family a new car.

Sitting across from her was a perfect way to start this journey. I wasn't as relaxed as I hoped, and I was probably too conscious of the nervous sweat beading on my forehead, but I did enjoy staring into Ellen's blue eyes. They were bright. I told her that I was ready to move on from Becca and Tia and hopefully find a future wife. She asked if I knew I was a virgin. I said yes, I did. And my plan for the fantasy suites? "You can do more than have sex," I said. "We could play board games, we could hang out."

Enough with the small talk. Ellen had a surprise planned.

"When do you meet the girls?" she asked.

"I think in a few days," I said.

"Actually, you're going to meet three of them in a minute," she said.

It was classic Ellen, and I was totally unprepared even though, earlier, I'd suspected something might be up when my *Bachelor* producer kept leaving my dressing room to speak with Ellen's producers. Now I knew. Three women were brought out: Sydney Lotuaco, Annie Reardon, and Katie Morton. I have no idea how these three were picked, but if I had to guess, it was their energetic personalities and TV-ready first impressions. They were fun, quick-witted, and cute.

We waved hello from afar while Ellen explained we were going to play Know or Go. The girls, who were standing on a raised platform, had to answer random questions Ellen and I threw at them. If they answered incorrectly, they disappeared through a trapdoor. The winner got to meet me, a tiny advantage in the race to win my heart.

At the end, Annie was the one still standing. She was a petite blonde who reminded me of Kate Hudson. She had a fun vibe. But Annie and I were only afforded enough time for a quick hello before Ellen cut to a commercial and Annie and the other two were taken backstage, and then I assume out of the studio, because I didn't see them again until the night of the first rose ceremony at the mansion.

Back in my dressing room, my producer wanted to know every thought and impression I had of those first three girls. I had a lot to say. Sydney had great legs. Was she a dancer? Annie was adorable in that cute little black top and harem pants, and I loved that she not only had seven dogs but that her mom kept them on a horse farm where they could run. She sounded cool. And Katie, wow, she looked fit and had a great sense of humor, and her description of a first date in Malibu hit a bull's-eye with me.

But before I was able to share any of those observations, I blurted out what was really on my mind: "Holy shit! That was fun!"

PART FOUR

How Do You Not Know?

My First Impressions

In my first twenty-four hours of life as the Bachelor, I experienced confusion, surprise, doubt, anger, tears, and excitement, and that was all before the first girl even got out of her limo. Here's the way it unfolded: First, I shot promotional videos with Jimmy Kimmel, who, before heading off to his own busy workday, wished me luck and said, "They're afraid if we spend any more time together you'll give me a rose."

Then I headed to a photoshoot with Chris Harrison. Though we hadn't spent much time together yet, I realized, as we sat next to each other in the makeup room, he knew me better than I thought.

"Relax," he said.

"I know, right?"

"Just let things happen," he said. "Don't stir the pot every time you get a chance to stir the pot. There will be a thousand little things that piss you off, and you're going to have to bite your tongue. Just trust us, trust yourself, and things will be fine."

It was vintage Chris: solid, practical advice from the man who provides the adult supervision that keeps everyone in line. Off camera, he was looser, much cooler. The next day I went to the mansion for my sit-and-chat interview with him. I was looking forward to having the time with him. It was the last piece of my intro package, and I knew it was going to set the tone for my season. It was my opportunity to acknowledge knowing that I wasn't everyone's first choice, but I still wanted to make the most of it.

Our talk went well. He asked some softball questions and allowed me to speak directly to fans in a way that I hoped endeared me to them. After we finished, I had an interview with *Entertainment Weekly* magazine's *Bachelor/Bachelorette* beat writer Kristen Baldwin. In a big coup for her, she had been given behind-the-scenes access to the premiere episode, including the opening night's rose ceremony. It was the first time a journalist had received permission to go anywhere and talk to everyone.

I had mixed feelings about meeting Kristen. She wasn't a fan of mine. She'd written some pretty nasty things about me. She'd taken some shots. All without having ever met me. Now was my chance to try to change her opinion. I wanted to charm her, if possible, and at the least give her a reason to not hate me. But sometimes, as I'd learned in my football career, writers don't change their opinions no matter what you say.

When we were introduced, she stuck out her hand and I went to hug her. I even said, "I'm a hugger. Give me a hug." She asked the easy, predictable questions first and then veered a little to the left. She complimented my teeth, asked how I planned to keep my energy up through the long night, and wondered what might happen if I fell in love with someone who didn't like dogs as much as I did. I got it—some quirky personal stuff. She was going for humor.

But then her tone changed. My answer about dogs didn't seem sufficient. She asked another question about me being *really* into dogs. Then she expressed concern about me seeming sad and perhaps putting too much pressure on myself. "I was personally concerned about you being the Bachelor," she said. "You seemed sad on *Paradise,* and it seemed like the best thing for you would be to go live off camera. I am concerned for your mental health."

Those questions and comments, by themselves, weren't that bad. It was the tone in which they were delivered. I felt like I was being mocked for . . . for what? Being sincere? Being open? Being honest?

I gave the show's publicist a look that said get me out of here. After one more question, I was free. Upset, I headed outside and straight to the black Suburban that had brought me to the mansion from the hotel. My producers followed me inside the car, where I chucked a water bottle against the front windshield and asked, "Why would you guys put me in that position? Do you not want me in a good headspace for this? After I told her that I was seeing a therapist, I felt like she made fun of me for that, or didn't take me seriously. I don't want to be ridiculed when I'm just being honest."

And I was. I'd already requested that the show have a therapist on-site. I'd started seeing a therapist when I played for the Oakland Raiders, and I was still an advocate of paying attention to mental-health issues, including my own. I wasn't 100 percent every day. Who is? That didn't make me less qualified for the show.

As I told Kristen, "You don't have to be a perfect person to deserve love. You don't have to be this perfect person to put yourself out there. And it's okay not to be perfect."

I went back to the hotel and changed clothes for the nighttime taping. The break allowed me to calm down, and by the time I returned to the mansion, word of the interview had gotten around and several producers came up to me and apologized. We taped my limo arrival quickly and without any glitches. I really enjoyed working with Chris. We wrapped the night by doing shots of Skrewball Whiskey, peanut butter–flavored booze that I brought to get us all off on a high note, and it worked.

Since it would be a long night, as I knew from *The Bachelorette*, I was reminded to stay up as late as possible and sleep in. "Try to reset your inner clock," I was told. I had more than enough thoughts and questions in my head to keep me awake well into the early hours of the next day. In fact, as I began to doze off, a little after 3:00 a.m., I remembered my dad had given me a journal before I left Denver. He wanted me to be able to document my journey. He'd written something on the first page, he told me, but he asked me not to read it until the first night.

Hey Bud—

Always remember I love you and I'm so very proud of you.
Don't forget . . .
To be present in the moment
To be open to something new
To be true to yourself
To go with your gut—it won't let you down
To always be respectful!
To enjoy every moment
To have fun!

I woke up later that day, between 1:00 and 2:00 p.m. A few hours later, I took a brief power nap, ran on the treadmill for about an hour, showered, and let Cary garb me in an outfit that, when I looked at myself in the mirror, put me in a state of thrilled disbelief. My suit was Hugo Boss, my tie was Gucci, and my shirt and shoes were of similar high-fashion lineage. I'm sure my wardrobe was equal to if not more than a couple months of my rent back home.

"This is stupid as shit," I crowed. "And I love it."

Then, in what seemed like a blink of my eyes, I was standing inside the gates shaking hands with Chris Harrison, as we'd done the previous night.

"Ready?" he asked.

It was 8:00 p.m., dark, with nearly a full moon overhead.

Between that and the lights, the grounds surrounding the mansion and the driveway leading up to it looked straight out of a fairy tale.

"Almost," I said.

I took a last-minute blast of breath spray before turning to Chris.

"Ready."

They had me do two takes walking up the driveway to meet Chris. After the second one, word echoed that we were good, which signaled Chris to turn to me and say, "Here's your first personal limo." It happened that fast. I swiveled slightly and saw Big Paulie striding up to the door of the first black car. Having been in the position once myself, I knew the instructions the stage manager was about to say to the person inside. As for me, there were no instructions, there was no script to follow, no safety net whatsoever.

It was time to see what would happen next . . .

The Long Night's
Journey into Love

"I haven't dated a virgin since I was twelve years old," said the first contestant out of the limo, Texas-based interior designer Demi Burnett.

As a memorable zinger, it worked. I laughed. I was also confused. What did she mean? Did *she* lose her virginity when she was twelve? Was she sexually active at thirteen?

Toronto realtor Caitlin Clemmens, breathing heavily in a tight red dress, used a needle to pop a red balloon. I didn't get the joke. I thought, what's she doing to that apple? But when she clarified—"Now that I popped your cherry, we don't need to talk about virginity anymore"—I thought, oh man, I'm going to get it every which way tonight. And I did.

Katie Morton used a deck of cards to illustrate the way she wanted to swipe my v-card. Alex Dillon dressed up like a sloth because, as she said, "I take things slow." Courtney Curtis asked if I had ever tasted a Georgia peach. I assumed that was a sexual innuendo of some sort, right? Even Chris Harrison, in his opening teaser, had asked if I might lose something in this twenty-third season of the show.

Although I expected the jokes about my virginity, I thought there were too many of them and warned producers it was annoyingly close to crossing the line. I didn't want the theme of the show to be let's get Colton laid. I also didn't want the audience to get bored. If you have a party and play the same song all night, people will get tired of it no matter how much they like the song. I suggested they keep the focus on romance and finding love.

I wasn't a TV producer, obviously, but I knew people watched for that simple reason. It was the reason I was on the show. Romance and love.

I had another issue that I kept to myself—or tried to until it became apparent later. I couldn't remember everyone's names. In football, the players had their names stitched onto the back of their uniform. As you got up after having the wind knocked out of you or worse, you didn't have to think, what's that big dude's name? I had no such crutches up at the mansion. The gowns were all backless, anyway.

Then I met someone who came with her own name tag, Caelynn Miller-Keyes. The former Miss USA runner-up wore a sash that read "Miss Underwood." Perfect. That was a name I'd practiced. She had a sparkle in her eyes and a smile that made me eager for our upcoming sit-down. Hannah Brown (Hannah B.) prompted a similar feeling of attraction. But hearing the former Miss Alabama gush "Roll Tide" as she did clashed with my Big Ten allegiance. If things worked out between us, we were going to have some heated Saturdays.

Cassie Randolph handed me a box and said that she had butterflies, meaning she was nervous, though she added that she also had actual butterflies. Then she spilled a box of fake butterflies in front of me. I put one in my pocket, while trying to hide the fact I was staring at her. I couldn't help it. And yes, she was cute and sexy, but what I noticed were her high heels. They had a Velcro strap and seemed practical, cool. She wasn't spending a month's salary on those heels with the red bottoms. I liked that about her.

I received a second box from Hannah Godwin (Hannah G.), who explained the box in her hand contained my favorite kind of underwear. It was empty. Ha-ha. She'd obviously watched *Paradise* and learned my preference for going commando. The joke made a good impression, as did she. Other gimmicks included Catherine Agro toting her Pomeranian, whose fluff let me know she'd also spent time in hair and makeup; Erin Landry arriving in a horse-drawn carriage; and Erika McNutt giving me a bag of nuts—easier to remember her name. I was also spoken to in Mandarin, Croatian, Spanish, and even a fake Australian accent.

Later, after four hours of introductions, it was time for the mix and mingle in the mansion. I'd lost track of how many energy drinks I'd gulped down, but it was clearly enough, as I had no problem getting the party started with an exuberant champagne toast. I had three main objectives for my one-on-one time with the women that night: make eye contact, laugh where appropriate, and try really hard to remember everyone's names. I remember the trouble Becca had; she'd forgotten Jason's name on our group date at the spa.

Apparently I was no better. Of all people, it was Cassie who busted me. We were walking past each other when she stopped and asked if I remembered her name. It was a sly move, but bold and forthright, and typical of Cass.

"No, I don't," I said, embarrassed.

Then I quickly reached into my jacket pocket and pulled out one of the fake butterflies she had given me earlier.

"But I have this from you."

Several other girls also asked if I knew their names. Some I did, and some I hemmed and hawed while sending a telepathic SOS to my producers. Brittany. Erika. Tracy. Onyeka. Allison. How could I remember all those names? I tried—I really did—and my forgetfulness was rude, but it was unintentional. I had just met thirty girls, more potential dates than I'd had in my entire life. Not only was I nervous, I was having the time of my life.

After every few girls, I was yanked into a nearby room for an interview with one of my producers. What did I think of the girls? Was there any attraction? Did I think I could lose my virginity to one of them? It was a little soon to talk about going all the way, but wow, as I said, I was having as much fun as I'd let myself imagine—maybe even more.

Even on sensory (and cocktail party conversation) overload, a few details stood out. Like Catherine interrupting numerous conversations and Onyeka fighting back for her time. I remembered Demi coming on strong. Katie was my first kiss. The second one with Caelynn was even better. Hannah B. was cool, too. What was it with me and beauty queens?

And then there was Cassie, a cute blond who was content to hang back and observe the other girls as they vied for my attention. In our one-on-one, I asked why she was on the show. It turned out to be a good story. Three years ago, she explained, she'd woken up from a vivid dream that she was on *The Bachelor*. She'd never seen the show before, but her dream was so real that she googled it and discovered there was a casting call for *The Bachelor* the next weekend near her Huntington Beach, California, home.

The timing was either weird or impeccable. Cassie went to the casting call and met with producers, who said she was exactly the sort of young woman they were looking for. Twice they invited her on the show, but Cass turned them down both times—the season with Nick Viall didn't work with her schedule, and she thought the next Bachelor, Arie Luyendyk, was a little too old for her. But the third time was the charm.

Why? Being in graduate school gave her more flexibility, and she was intrigued by the new Bachelor himself, namely me. That put a smile on my face. Who wouldn't like hearing that? But she didn't say any more on that topic, at least not then. More would come out later on. Cass was smart and careful with what she said.

It was all good. At nearly 5:00 a.m., I gave out the night's first big prize, the first impression rose. Initially, I wanted to give it to Caelynn. We'd had a good follow-up chat outside and seemed to connect right away, especially with our kiss. However first impressions are measured, I didn't see it getting any better than Caelynn. Then, in my ITM and additional conversations with my producers, I wondered if the all-American football player giving his first rose to the Miss USA 2018 runner-up was too cliché for the opening episode.

Sometimes I tend to overthink situations, and this was one of those cases. After some internal deliberations and a strong desire to make this season premiere the best ever, I gave my first impression rose to Hannah G. She reminded me of home, I explained. By that, I meant I felt comfortable around her. She was safe.

What did I know about anything at this point except I was nervous as hell—and tired and maybe even a little punchy from being up all night. But I knew there were no wrong choices if I paid attention to my instincts, and my instincts told me that Caelynn and Hannah G. both made fine first impressions. I had to trust the process, as Chris Harrison had advised. The producers knew what they were doing. They cast the show with intent and insight. After rounds of interviews, they knew the thirty women as well as the women knew themselves and their goal in bringing them on was the same as mine: an engagement and marriage.

Out of the thirty contestants that night, I think five or six were picked especially for me. They were the likely matches, the maybe-she-might-be-the-future Mrs. Underwood. The rest were strong, colorful personalities, with a couple of question marks, a couple of possibilities, a couple of you-never-knows, and a few unpredictable wild cards.

I wanted to send Kirpa Sudick home. She was very attractive, but I wanted more connection with people than just appearances. Her hello didn't work, and our short sit-down fell flat. My producer liked Kirpa and advised me not to judge her harshly.

"She had an off night," Nancy said. "Just give her some time."

I was already giving Sydney Lotuaco time to prove herself. One of the three girls who were on *Ellen*, she tried to teach me to dance in our first one-on-one out on the driveway, with a string quartet playing "Clair de Lune," and in the midst of that ambitious effort, I figured out that she was the NBA dancer a buddy of mine in PR had mentioned in a text before my phone got taken away: "One of my girls, Sydney, just got confirmed to be on your show," he wrote. "Take care of her."

I didn't sense any sparks between us, but Sydney seemed cool, so I thought why not keep her around until it didn't make sense? I did the same with Kirpa. Both of them got roses. So did Demi and Catherine, two others who were borderlines that night. They'd annoyed me, but what if it was nerves and I was missing out on something good?

Even now, looking back, I felt bad judging people without getting to know them. In real life, if I meet someone new and it's off for one reason or another, I turn and leave. I don't send them away. Only on TV do you have that power, and it's not always comfortable. But ultimately, because it was my job, I did not give roses to Alex Dillon, Devin Gooden, Erin Landry, Adrianne Averbukh, Laura Pellerito, Revian Chang, and Tahzjuan Hawkins.

Sorry, ladies, at this point, it was nothing personal. We probably didn't have enough time to connect, and I didn't want to waste anyone's time.

The morning sun was already up when the last roses were handed out. I was utterly drained from this marathon. Everyone else was dragging, too. I tried not to overthink the decisions I didn't make or regret the ones I did. There were still twenty-three girls to focus on, another couple hours of wrap-up interviews to do, and . . . three more months ahead of me. As I poured sweetener in a cup of coffee, a producer asked how I was doing. I looked at him, surprised it wasn't evident. I was as tired as I'd ever been in my life, but in the best possible way, and feeling so lucky I could hardly believe this was really happening to me.

The all-American kid.

Me next to our
Disney-decorated tree.
I'm wearing onesie PJs,
which I still love and
occasionally wear.

Connor (right), my dad, and me
on photo day in football. I was in
seventh grade and didn't like the
way I looked in a uniform.

Connor (right) and me showing off the latest cool hairstyles of 2007 in Washington, Illinois.

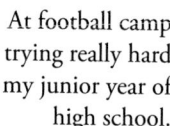

At football camp trying really hard my junior year of high school.

My mom and me before
I went to a rock band–themed
dance junior year of high school.

Me as a high school junior with a fresh catch from our backyard pond.

High school
graduation
with my
mom and dad.

Connor at Indiana State with
my mom and me.

My cousin Harper, then one year
old, whose cystic fibrosis inspired
me to start the Colton Underwood
Legacy Foundation.

My mom and me on a hike.

My mom and me shortly after she and my dad divorced; he took the picture and we all had a good dinner together. They're both good sports.

Looking like a football player on the sidelines with the Chargers.

Catching a pass
against the
Arizona Cardinals
despite intense
shoulder pain.

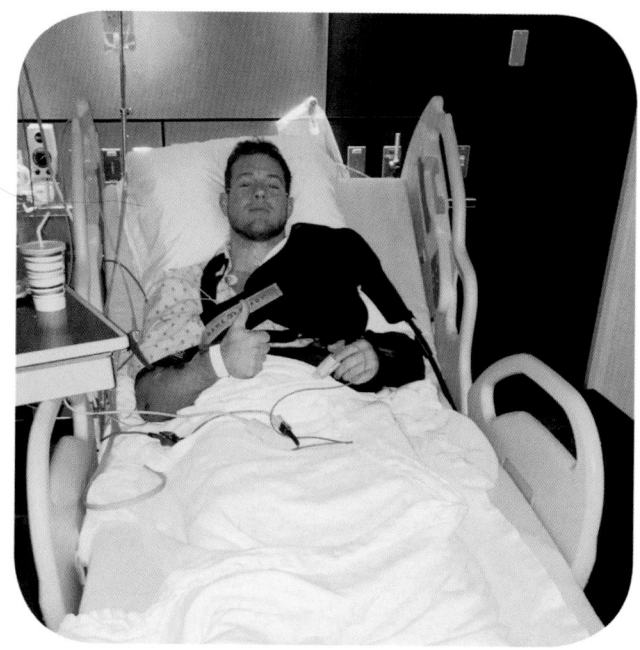

Shoulder surgery
in Colorado.

Me in the kitchen at the mansion on *The Bachelorette*.
To start the day, I was making avocado toast.

Becca and me on a catamaran in the
Bahamas before she found out
I was a virgin.

Becca and Robbie showing
me some affection.

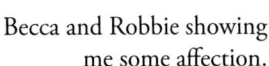

My dad, Connor, and me on the morning Connor got married in the Dominican Republic. That same day, the episode aired on which I told Becca I was a virgin.

My first date with Tia on *Bachelor in Paradise*. Through all the drama, we've stayed friends.

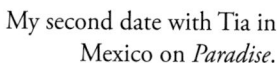

My second date with Tia in Mexico on *Paradise*.

On *GMA*, the morning I was announced as the Bachelor. (I look serious because I'm watching the replay of my highlights and lowlights from *The Bachelorette* and *Bachelor in Paradise*.)

Definitely not traveling light as the Bachelor, with Penny Egan, one of my producing angels.

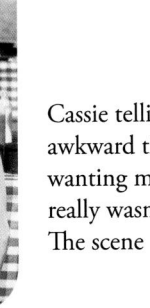

Cassie telling me she was awkward the first night and wanting me to know she really wasn't like that—duh. The scene didn't air.

Enjoying a sunset over
the water in the Bahamas.

Beach run in
Thailand.

Enjoying a sunset over the water in the Bahamas.

Cass and me starting the fantasy early in Spain after we went rock climbing.

Cass and me gone Hollywood, smiling in a photo booth at a party.

My third appearance on *Ellen*. My secret? I wear *Ellen* underwear when
I go on the show. (I also stole that coffee mug.)

Taking a selfie on a plane.

Beach day in Huntington Beach. Cass stole my hat; this is proof.

On a ski trip to Aspen with my rescue dog, Thor, who lives with my mom and my bonus dad, Dan.

Cass playing hard to kiss at a Denver fund raiser for the Legacy Foundation.

Cozy next to the fire pit on a chilly LA night.

Cass and me with her sister, Michelle, and Michelle's boyfriend, Gregg Sulkin, at Stagecoach in 2019.

Enjoying
country music—
and each other—
at Stagecoach.

On my birthday in
our Happy Couple
home.

In love.

It didn't happen often, but there were a few times over the three months of shooting that walkies crackled with the news flash, "We've got an emergency ten-three. Bachelor is hangry."

The Long Night's Journey into Love (Continued)

When I got back to my hotel room, I changed into a T-shirt and sweats and prepared to tackle what would be my final task every night I was the Bachelor. I took a handful of deep breaths, cleared my head, opened my heart, and thought about all the women I'd met or interacted with earlier in the day. Who were my favorites? Who was a maybe? Who did I look forward to seeing again? Who was not in the running?

I coveted this quiet time for the opportunity it gave me to process the conversations I'd had with the different girls and the ways I felt about them. The days were so jam-packed with activities and interviews that there wasn't any free time to think—or feel. Love is many things, including that mysterious way people react when there is chemistry. "Who are you?"

You can't stop thinking about someone and if asked why, you don't really know why, you just can't stop yourself. But it might be fleeting, and you don't want to miss it, which will happen if you don't pay attention. And so there I was, in T-shirt and sweats, thinking about all those girls, which was not an unpleasant task.

My top five were Hannah G., Caelynn, Tayshia Adams, Hannah B., and Annie Reardon. I doubted all of them would stay on the list or that it would remain in that order, but it worked for me after this long first night and I made a mental note to relay my favorites to my producers the next morning, as would be my routine almost to the end of production. What else were we going to talk about?

The funny thing was, once I got into bed and my head finally hit the pillow, I was still thinking about which girls were my favorites and I started to redo some of my original choices. I realized that I'd forgotten one girl who deserved to be at or near the very top; and now I couldn't stop thinking about her. I'd forgotten her name earlier. How'd she slip my mind again? I laughed to myself and bet I wouldn't forget her ever again.

Episode Two— What No One Saw

COLTON'S ANGELS

The following afternoon I met with my producers. The team— Nancy, Eileen, and Penny. Or, as I nicknamed them, Colton's Angels. They were my pillars throughout the season: guiding and support- ing me when I needed it and offering assistance even when I thought I had things under control. What I learned? I never had things under control. And never ignore a well-meaning woman's advice.

These three women were a formidable, impressive group whose talents complimented each other. Nancy was mission-oriented. Eileen was my free-spirited sister who would be able to open me up in an interview like no one else. And Penny was a sparkplug of a human being, all spirit and emotion, who just loved love.

I was eager to sit down with them and recap that first rose cer- emony. I felt like the host of a big party; I wanted to hear it went well. They were pleased. We gossiped about the previous night and talked about all the girls, who were at that moment moving into the mansion. They reviewed the schedule for the rest of the week, which was crazy busy and included my first one-on-one date with Hannah B. That put a smile on my face.

I was less enthusiastic about the first group date: a trip to the theater where husband-and-wife actors Megan Mullally and Nick Offerman would headline a night of telling stories about our "firsts." Each person could define for themselves what so-called first time in their life they wanted to talk about, though I knew what it meant for me.

Nancy saw me roll my eyes. The point, she said, was for me to address what she referred to as "the elephant in the room."

"I have to think that elephant is pretty tired by now," I said.

I heard Chris in my head: *pick your battles*. Grumpy but ultimately agreeable, I did my part the next day at the theater. Megan and Nick warmed up the audience with some risqué stories about their own first sexual experiences. I stuck to the "First Comes Love" theme of the show by recalling the time I stood up in front of a squad of San Diego Charger linebackers and revealed I was a virgin. Ay-yai-yai, I was glad that was done.

I'M SORRY, I SUCK AT THIS

Hannah and I climbed into a battered old Jeep eager to get to know each other on the forty-five-minute drive to Vasquez Rocks in the mountains north of LA. Excited about this first one-on-one date, we were mic'd and seated in front of a GoPro camera positioned to capture us getting to know each other. I kept glancing at her, hoping to see if she was enjoying herself. I was nervous. I think she was, too. Was this what I missed out on in high school by not dating?

We saved most of our conversation until we were at Vasquez Rocks, which was tough considering how eager both of us were to ask questions and share details about our lives. But then it was game on. It was Hannah's birthday, and I wanted her to have a good time. She made me feel good by saying the date was a great present. We rode horses through the dramatic desert scenery until we arrived at a strategically placed hot tub, which was a perfect setup for a very happy birthday celebration.

After changing into swimsuits, we got in the hot tub and opened a bottle of champagne that was chilled and waiting for us. Both of us were smiling, getting into the vibe. I went through the process of forgetting I was on a TV show; as far as I was concerned, it was just me and Hannah, surrounded by bubbles and ready to sip glasses full of stars. Everything was perfect—that is, until I suggested she make a toast. I saw her eyes fill with fear. I knew what was happening to her. Her mind went blank. She lost it. The poor thing froze.

"I'm sorry, I suck at this," she said.

I felt bad for her. I tried to help.

"Don't look at the cameras," I advised. "Just talk to me."

I understood what was going on with her. From the beginning of our date, Hannah was more concerned with how she looked on camera—her hair, the light, the camera angles, the sound—than anything else. She paid attention to every little detail except the most important one: enjoying herself. To succeed on this show, you had to ignore everything around you: the cameras, the producers, the sound people running wires down your back or inside your pants, the competition, and the show itself. Hannah did the opposite, and she was overwhelmed by all of it, until she was paralyzed.

"Take a moment," her producer said.

I wished she would've stayed in the moment, too. As a way of getting herself together, though, she fell back on questions she'd prepared earlier. She asked about my decision to remain a virgin and followed that with one about my relationship with Aly.

"I know you used to date Aly Raisman," she said. "Why don't you ever talk about that relationship?"

She had done her homework, and I suppose there would've been nothing wrong with that question if we'd known each other better and didn't have cameras pointed at us. But our situation wasn't either of those and she saw my face curdle in the wake of her query. I explained that the producers and I had agreed to keep mention of her off-limits.

"Got it," she said.

I liked Hannah, but in my first ITM assessment I said she needed to loosen up. We were scheduled to have dinner later that night aboard the *Queen Mary* in Long Beach, and I urged the producers to encourage her to talk to me instead of the people behind the camera. She needed some friendly coaching, which apparently she received. In a beauty pageant, you're modeling; on *The Bachelor*, you have to be yourself. To her credit, Hannah pulled herself together for the dinner portion of the date and was a thoroughly enjoyable companion—clever, inquisitive, bright, beautiful, and totally deserving of the rose she received.

CASSIE WANTS TO TALK TO YOU ABOUT SOMETHING

For the week's second group date, twelve girls were divided into two teams for a day of games and competitions. The winning team got an overnight with me. Comedian Billy Eichner was called in to provide the commentary. This activity was more my speed than a night of embarrassing confessions at the theater. During a break in the action, one of my producers walked over to me with a second producer. He worked with Cassie, the blond from Huntington Beach. She wanted to pull me for a private conversation, he said.

I asked if everything was okay. Neither producer commented one way or the other.

"Have the conversation," my producer said.

Soon Cassie and I were walking to a bench where we could talk by ourselves. I liked her confidence. She looked me in the eye and said she was concerned about the impression she made—or didn't make—when we talked at the cocktail party the first night. "I felt a little off and I want to let you know I'm normally pretty outgoing," she said. "But sometimes I struggle. And with that whole situation and everything being new and unfamiliar, I felt like I was awkward and I don't want you to think I'm awkward. So I just wanted to clear the air."

I assured Cassie that nothing about her or our conversation that night had been awkward. "Good," she said, without offering anything else but leaving the door open for me to keep the conversation going if I wanted, which I very much did.

I was delighted to get to know her and see that she grew more comfortable as we talked. She'd played soccer and volleyball in high school. She'd attended Biola University, a Christian school about an hour from her home. She liked board games. With a tiny bit of embarrassment, she said that she'd watched Becca's season of *The Bachelorette* and her friends and family were a little obsessed with me.

"That's why I started blushing halfway through our introduction," she said.

"You did?" I said.

"Yeah, I was thinking, I could like this guy." She smiled.

I wanted to kiss her right then, but she was pulled away before I could muster the courage. It was probably for the better. Good things shouldn't be rushed, right?

I kept my eye on her the rest of the afternoon as the girls were divided into red and yellow teams and competed in various events, including a canoe race and tug-of-war that ultimately decided who won the overnight with me. The red team, which happened to have all my favorites, emerged victorious. It gave me more time with Cassie, who, it turned out, had a first kiss on her mind, too.

Later that night, as we sat around the campfire, she orchestrated an egg-and-spoon game for just the two of us. She planned to drop the spoon from her mouth as she passed the egg from her spoon to mine and kiss me. The idea was as cute as her. But I screwed it up.

When she turned around after getting the egg and spoons, I was standing right behind her and . . . I'll just say we will never have to wonder which came first, the kiss or the egg.

A WORD ABOUT KISSING LOTS OF GIRLS

This may shock you, but I was fine with it. I was aware that on *The Bachelorette*, I was kind of skeeved out on group dates with Becca when I was the second, third, or fourth guy kissing her. Now, standing on the other side, I had no such qualms. Was I guilty of a double standard? Yes. Was I apologetic? No. But I was sensitive when Heather, at that night's campfire, informed me that she was not only a virgin but she'd never kissed a boy. She received the group-date rose for her courage and honesty, and both of us knew that down the road, when the time was right, we'd wade into virgin territory and kiss.

DEMI SCARED ME

I had no idea the cocktail party would be the equivalent of a bartender calling, "Last round." I saw Demi coming toward me wearing a white terry-cloth bathrobe with God only knew what was—or wasn't—underneath it. I tried to hide my unease with her behavior as she tore me away from Tracy Shapoff and took me upstairs to her so-called fantasy closet for a private massage. She intimidated me. When I met girls like her in high school and college, I ran in the opposite direction. She forced me out of my comfort zone. Such things would've never happened to the Bachelorette. She had to always be in control. A different standard was applied to me. I wasn't aware of people commenting on this, if they did. I had a cherry popped in my face. I was propositioned. In the end, I suppose it was my call, and I was okay with it. I trusted my producer angels to never let things go too far or to hear me if I said I was too uncomfortable.

WE HAVE A PROBLEM

In a meeting with my producers mid-week, Nancy intimated that someone in the house was stirring up trouble. They were keeping an eye on her, they said. I'd heard rumors about conflict between Caelynn and Hannah B. I knew some of the girls with pageant backgrounds had speculated they weren't BFFs anymore, but whatever additional details were floating around had escaped my ears, and I was assured that neither of them was the problem anyway.

With my concerns alleviated, I left the behind-the-scenes kerfuffle to production and went to the cocktail party. Demi came down in a bathrobe and gave me a massage in a closet, which had the opposite effect of relaxing me. I think there were more sex jokes cracked in the room that night than bottles of white wine. Onyeka blasted an air horn and declared she was horny. Then Sydney came into the room pounding a spoon on a pot. Was that a joke about banging? My head was spinning from all the clamor that night.

The four girls who came up short in the next rose ceremony were Annie Reardon, Alex Blumberg, Erika McNutt, and Angelique Sherman.

Afterward, in my hotel room, I sat up questioning myself: I saw the possibility that at the end of this I could definitely fall in love and even lose my virginity, but I wondered if *Entertainment Weekly*'s Kristen Baldwin might have been right: Would I be making decisions due to the pressure of being on a TV show and wanting to please people, or because the emotions I felt were genuine? How would I know for sure? I had a lot to figure out on my own.

But few secrets stayed secret for very long on *The Bachelor.* If there was a rumor, trouble, an argument, an outburst, or hurt feelings, it got out and traveled fast.

Tension

Midway through the third week the rift between Caelynn and Hannah B. exploded into the open and turned the former Miss USA roommates into fierce and unfriendly competitors. Both came to me talking smack about each other, and I hated it. From what they told me off camera, their problem had to do with a tasteless joke about a serious matter related to one of their family members. I won't say anything more. The tension of being on the show together opened this old wound and cast a dark cloud over the entire week.

I know my team picked up on my disappointment and it didn't improve as we set forth into the week's events. We started with a themed dinner at a place called Pirates Adventure, where the main course was a jousting match between—surprise, surprise—Caelynn and Hannah B. Caelynn won and the crowd chanted, "Kiss her! Kiss her!" I complied with a congratulatory peck on Caelynn's cheek. I sensed the crowd, the producers, and even Caelynn wanted more PDA, but I resisted. I was uncomfortable making out in front of the other girls. Seeing Becca kiss other guys had bothered me on *The Bachelorette*, and I wanted to spare others now that I had lips in the game. It was hard enough just knowing people were smooching when you couldn't see it.

My one-on-one date was with Elyse. The redheaded makeup artist was a knockout with intense eyes, a friendly smile, and an interesting life in the Arizona desert that she was looking to share with someone special. I knew it wasn't going to be me. Unfortunately for Elyse, I was impatient and frustrated by not getting time with my favorites, like Hannah G. I was ready to fall in love. Why no dates with her?

I pressed my team of angels. What was going on?

It was only week three and I didn't want to come off like a prima donna, but I'm a pretty direct person and try not to waste time when there is a problem. I liked Hannah G., and I was eager to see if the attraction was real or an infatuation I'd manufactured. We hadn't spent that much time together, but she checked off all the boxes. So did Caelynn, who intrigued me from day one. And so did Cassie, who was constantly in my thoughts.

What about her? My team asked.

Yeah, what about her. It wasn't a question. Did they not see what was obvious to me? Cassie was cool. Period.

I wanted one-on-ones with all of those girls ASAP. But like the song says, you can't always get what you want. You get what you need.

The week's second group event was the Bachelor's Strongest Women competition hosted by actor and former pro football player Terry Crews and his wife, Rebecca King-Crews, in downtown Los Angeles. The actual competition was outdoors, but we warmed up in a sleek, modern gym where I helped several of the girls loosen up, including Sydney, who, as a professional dancer, made a point of showing me how limber she was. It caught the attention of Cassie, who said, "Colton's not a stretching virgin anymore, that's for sure."

Everyone was on a high at the cocktail party later that night. It was staged at the brand-new Metropolis complex nearby, a group of sleek high-rise condos that towered above the city with extraordinary views. The show had secured a penthouse on the thirty-eighth floor for me to use as a getaway to rest and refresh, and during a break I took Cassie up there to share the spectacular setting with her.

We sat down on a sofa and let the views out the floor-to-ceiling windows lull us into a place of relaxation and closeness. We felt like we were floating above the world, just the two of us. It was light, easy, and intimate. As we talked and kissed, I fidgeted with one of her rings, absent-mindedly tugging at it and spinning it. Once I realized what I was doing, I looked at the ring and noticed it read, "JEREMIAH 29:11."

"That's amazing," I said.

"What?" she asked.

"Your ring. It's got the Bible verse I try to live by."

"Jeremiah 29:11," she said.

" '*For I know the plans I have for you,*' declares the Lord, '*plans to prosper you, not to harm you, plans to give you—*' "

" '*Hope and a future,*' " she chimed in.

"Exactly," I said.

Back at the mansion, we sought to chill prior to the rose ceremony with a pool party. Only there was nothing relaxing about Hannah B. and Caelynn. Their feud was reaching a boiling point. First, Hannah B. took me aside and said, "I just don't understand how you can be into her and still be into me. We're just so different." Then, as I walked with Caelynn for some equal-opportunity private time, Hannah B. confided to Heather, "If Caelynn's talking crap about me, she better beware. There's a monster inside of me."

Caelynn was no pushover. After getting situated on a bench, she leaned forward and said, "Okay, let's get into it." According to Caelynn, her friendship with Hannah B. fell apart when she began to have more success at the Miss USA competition. There was, she said, "manipulation, deceitfulness, and talking not kind things about me. It's such a pattern of behavior, and you can see it in the house."

My eyes glazed over. In my ITM, I said, "This makes me sick to my stomach." I liked both of these women and didn't want their problems spoiling my time. I told my producers it was a problem that needed to be addressed and solved. Hoping that I might be able to broker a peace between these one-time friends, I sat down again with Hannah B., who said Caeylnn was manipulative and phony and she warned me to be wary of her. "I honestly believe if you picked her at the end you'd never see the full person."

The name-calling didn't sit well with me. Neither did I believe it. I thought Hannah's attack was probably the result of hurt feelings or a misunderstanding that could be talked through if given the opportunity. I wanted to speak with Caelynn, but she wasn't available.

After a break, Chris Harrison questioned me about the Hannah B. and Caelynn feud. I assured him their bad blood wouldn't affect my decisions in the rose ceremony. I thought their situation could be worked out and their friendship resumed regardless of my future with either one of them. We'd have to see.

I had a much better time at the pool party with Cassie. We picked up where we'd left off at the Metropolis. Later, both of us remembered this as the time we realized how easy it was to spend time together. She was easygoing, natural, and sweet-natured. There was nothing phony about her. We had a natural rapport. Conversation flowed between us. Her voice sounded like music to me. I kept pressing Play. I wanted to hear everything about her life.

She was generous with details. From a close family, she was the oldest of three children raised by her marketing executive dad, Matt, and her mom, Amy. Her younger sister, Michelle, was an actress-model, and her brother, Landon, was still in high school. They were all blond and athletic. She surfed and felt best when she was doing anything outdoors. She was enjoying the experience of being on the show thus far, but she had concerns about putting her life out there on a show as popular as *The Bachelor*.

"I don't know if I'm ready for my life to be out there," she said. "Or if I even want it to be out there. Being judged by everyone. Having people talk about me on social media. It seems weird. I like simple things. I like my quiet little life."

Cassie suggested we play two truths and a lie. It would be an entertaining way for us to learn about each other, she said. Cass also loves games—board games, cards, and two truths and a lie. She went first and told me that she had two cats named Goose and Maverick, a degree in communication sciences and disorders, and her pilot's license. As she shared those facts, I searched her face for the slightest indication of a fib. I didn't see a single quiver. She was good.

I had to make an educated guess. Since my passion for dogs was well-known, I thought she was probably lying about having two cats. Cassie laughed and said, "Nope, the cats are real. They're my babies."

"This is crushing," I said, with a troubled laugh. "You can't have cats. You're perfect."

"Sorry."

"Well, good luck getting a rose," I said, laughing.

I ran into Caelynn later that afternoon. I saw she was still upset. I tried to soothe any concerns she might have had and told her she was brave.

"I really do have a lot to tell you about my past," she said, as her eyes filled with tears again.

"We'll talk about it later," I said, in a tone meant to comfort. "You're going to be around for a while."

I knew one or two conversations weren't going to solve everyone's problems, but there was good news that would help. We were traveling to Singapore and neighboring countries. A change of scenery was going to be good for everything. I couldn't wait or contain my excitement. I had never traveled anywhere as far or exotic as Singapore. I was also traveling with some very cool young women who I wanted to get to know better. I assumed that once there, I'd finally get one-on-one dates with Hannah G., Caelynn, Cassie, and others.

Even better, I didn't have to pack. It was all done for me. I was truly having the time of my life and I imagined it was only going to get better.

Past Lives, Present Tense

The first thing I saw as we approached Singapore was the flight attendant. I was waking up in my comfortable first-class seat, and he was looking down at me the way a surgeon might after giving up on a patient for dead and then seeing him flutter and miraculously open his eyes. Grinning, the flight attendant clasped his hands together and exclaimed, "I've never had anyone sleep fifteen hours before. What did you take?"

"Nothing," I said, maneuvering my seat into an upright position. "I spent the last three weeks dating thirty women. I'm exhausted."

My producer, seated nearby, exploded in laughter. But this extreme fatigue was a necessary by-product of the gig. No pain, no gain. Soon after checking into the hotel, I was outside with a production crew, gathering B-roll for a new intro package highlighting the sights of this faraway city. I guzzled energy drinks to battle the jet lag. I was in awe. I didn't want to miss a sight, smell, or taste of anything.

My first solo date there was with Tayshia, one of the women who most intrigued me. If there was a wild card among my favorites, it was Tayshia, a phlebotomist from Corona del Mar, California. We hadn't talked as extensively as I had with some of the other girls, but I had taken note of her the past few weeks. I knew she had a strong sense of faith and commitment to helping other people. I'd been privy to her sense of humor and her attitude toward having fun on the show. I knew we could be good friends.

Our date was an unexpected bonding experience. We went bungee jumping. I wished I could've been more excited about the activity, and I expressed what for me passed as great enthusiasm in front of the cameras, but I can't emphasize enough how much I hate heights. I get queasy looking down from the second story at the shopping mall. Tayshia abhorred the sensation of falling. We were a perfect twosome for this date; I didn't know about Tayshia, but I was almost guaranteed to freak out. At the same time, we were confronting our fears and hopefully learning we could not only survive them but also grow, which was one of the elements that made this show successful.

This date also provided an apt metaphor for getting into a relationship—and an opportunity for bad puns. As we walked along the beach, the white scaffolding of the Bungy tower ahead of us, I asked Tayshia if she was ready to *fall* in love. It would be our *leap of faith*. Ha-ha, right? Standing one thousand feet above the ground, Tayshia and I made a pact: "Let's just go have a good, fun time." She added, "Don't die. Have fun."

Later that night, dinner was in a fancy restaurant at the top of a towering hotel, where Tayshia and I enjoyed a window table with a breathtaking view of the city. I asked about her background in biology and missionary work with her church. She opened up about being divorced and wanting to have a successful, loving relationship. I gave her a rose and we ended our date with champagne and a kiss as we enjoyed the spectacular nighttime view from the Singapore Flyer, one of the world's largest Ferris wheels.

But I was falling in love with Cassie. I sensed it during our group date touring Singapore's Chinatown. It was me and thirteen remaining girls. We engaged in some of the local customs, like leech therapy, shopped in the outdoor markets, and sampled food. I know this segment received criticism for promoting stereotypes. I think the intention was to celebrate the culture, which we did.

Singapore is home to some of the world's best street food, and while frogs and pigs' feet may be too much for some of us to handle, we tried it. Yes, it made some people squeamish. But those reactions weren't intended as put-downs. I think it would've been a bigger slight to have not tried anything.

Cassie and I visited a fortune-teller who said we had been brother and sister in a previous life. We jokingly wondered if that made kissing in this life incestuous. I quickly dismissed that thought as semigross and silly. "So we're good?" Cass asked. "We're good," I said.

Very good, in fact. Whenever I was around Cass that afternoon, I tried to get close to her and let her know that I liked her very much. I touched her back, tapped her on the shoulder, or put my arm around her. I tried to keep it subtle. I did the same thing with Hannah G., maybe not as much, but I wanted to send her a similar message.

I was a busy boy. After giving Demi the group-date rose and a long, serious talk with Hannah B. that got us back on track, I asked producers if I could have a little alone time with Cassie. I knew our next destination was Thailand and wanted to continue my efforts to get her ready for a one-on-one. I guess I was making progress. They checked with her, and she said yes. We had an amazing time together. Her dress was even more amazing—and pure Cass, right up to the line of *Oh my God* but still tasteful.

Alone and sipping white wine, we laughed again about being brother and sister in a past life, and I about called it game over when she said, "I feel like I've been trying all day to get you." Then, after a few minutes of making out, she flashed a naughty smile and laughed. "Would your sister kiss you like that?"

Damn.

That night I had my first solid, uninterrupted sleep of the trip and woke up feeling fresh and normal. All the jet lag was finally behind me and I was ready for my second one-on-one date of the trip, this time with Caelynn, one of my favorites. Given what she'd started to tell me back in the States about having been sexually assaulted in college, I knew this was going to be an emotional date. But Caelynn looked buoyant and happy when we got together that afternoon. We shared a delicious lunch and went shopping.

I found out she'd been to Singapore only five months earlier. She'd broken up with her ex-boyfriend there. "So lots of good memories in Singapore," I said facetiously. She assured me that she was over the breakup and enjoying being back in the city. I wondered if she was over everything.

"Are you okay?" I asked. "You don't really have to talk about it. Whatever you want to share. It's up to you."

Caelynn assured me she was prepared to recount the ordeal despite worries about the way people might react once the show aired. She wouldn't ever put the abuse fully behind her, she explained, but she'd done the work required to move forward in her life and she wanted to serve as a cautionary tale to other women. I promised whatever support she needed. Having been in a relationship with a survivor of sexual assault, I'd seen some of the struggle and extraordinary resolve it took to go public.

Later that night, as Caelynn sat opposite me at the dinner table, I saw in her the strength and conviction of someone ready to share her very painful truth. This was the most serious issue the Bachelor franchise had ever addressed. Producers created an environment that felt safe, personal, and comfortable. They warned crew members of a potentially triggering conversation and gave them the option to excuse themselves.

After we exchanged a few pleasantries to help her settle in,

Caelynn opened up about having been sexually assaulted after a fraternity party in college. This "real-life shit," as she called it, had happened four years earlier and left her "deeply hurt," which I was sure didn't come close to describing the scars she'd have for the rest of her life. The details she described were graphic and horrible and don't need to be repeated. What does need to be mentioned again, I think, is that the local hospital where she first sought help refused to provide her with a rape kit and none of her attackers were prosecuted.

I was incensed when she recalled that part. Women need to be believed and helped. Period. "It's so painful and it screws up every ounce of you," she said.

"I want you to know that with me, you're safe," I said, as I'd once told Aly. "I can't even imagine going through something like that. I know talking about it is not easy. The fact that it happened to you is devastating." In the rawness of the moment, I acknowledged having been in a relationship with someone who'd been sexually abused. I said the hardest thing I ever had to do was to look "into her eyes" and see "the pain associated with it."

"I think that's one thing people never understand is the intimacy that goes along with what you've experienced, and I've been on the other side of it," I said. "And for me, for that to be my first love and the first person I found for me and it didn't happen . . ."

Afterward, Caelynn, who was clearly emotionally drained, took a rose from me and held it gently as we got up from the table. We went for a brief walk through the park, away from the cameras, to unwind. When the episode aired a few months later, the network provided resources for those affected by sexual abuse, including the number for RAINN, the national sexual assault hotline (800-656-4673). Aly praised her, too. "I am supportive of anybody that comes forward and especially for her to do that on national television," she told *People* magazine. "I really commend her for her bravery and I stand with her and I hope she's getting a ton of support because she deserves it."

My sentiments exactly. Back in my hotel room, I reflected admiringly on the strength and courage Caelynn had summoned to tell her story. The night had definitely bonded us in a way I never expected. I was concerned about having talked about my past relationship, in the sense that Aly's story wasn't mine to share. But there was value in talking about being in a relationship with someone working to recover. You don't ever want to see people hurting, and when they are you want to be there to help.

Caelynn's confession seemed to have a cleansing effect on everyone. The next day, she and Hannah B. repaired their relationship and decided to be friends again. I finally got one-on-one time with Hannah G., which confirmed the status I held her in my head and my heart. Everything was hunky-dory, that is until Elyse started pining for more attention. She handed me a note, which I turned over to producers and let them deal with her frustrations at not spending more time with me.

I was happy with the way things were turning out. In the rose ceremony that buttoned our excursion to Singapore, I sent Courtney and Tracy home. Later that night, as I sat in my hotel room pondering my favorites and thinking about what I wanted to tell my producers the next day, I couldn't help reflecting on my crazy good fortune at being the Bachelor. I pictured Hannah G., Cassie, Caelynn, and the others and wondered whether I ever would have met these amazing young women if not for the show.

How did I get so lucky?

What happened in the universe to align the stars in my favor?

Why did God choose to answer my prayers?

Not that many years earlier I'd gone to the junior-senior prom in high school with Hilary Rose, a senior. I was a sophomore. She only asked me after breaking up with her boyfriend. I was hardly

Bachelor material back then. I rented a white tux, white shirt, white shoes, and a teal-colored tie and pocket square. Everything was way too big and unfitted. I had the style of a telephone pole—and a really bad haircut.

It got worse. Unbeknownst to me, Hilary had recently gotten back together with her boyfriend and she ditched me at the dance before the band played their first song. I left early. But look at me now. Life was certainly funny and even more unpredictable.

On to Thailand.

What I Knew in Thailand

Morning in Thailand. We were at a Robinson Club luxury beach resort in Khao Lak. Outside my window, past the palm trees, the pools, and the white-sand beaches, was water so blue and inviting it looked fake. I stared out the window and found myself thinking about Cassie. She'd been on my mind when I'd woken up and she was still on my mind. As I drank my coffee, I wondered what she was doing. I couldn't wait to see her.

"The funny thing is, I never put her as my number one," I said to Cary, the show's head of wardrobe and my pseudo shrink.

My first appointment of the day was with him, to go through some of my wardrobe for Thailand. As I looked at shirts and bathing suits, I told him how this infatuation of mine had turned into something more serious. I told him how I liked visiting with the other girls, even kissing some of them (because hey, why not, it was my job as the Bachelor), but I realized that more and more often I was either waiting to see Cassie or thinking about seeing her.

"I haven't had a one-on-one with her yet," I continued. "I am so freaking ready to spend time alone with that girl."

Cary was silent, as he always was.

"Is that how love happens?" I mused. "You just wake up one day and you know?"

I told him that Hannah G. had been my number one from the beginning. But I was having doubts about her. Though she checked all the boxes, as I'd said before, I wondered if she was challenging enough. If we were in a relationship, would she push me in all the ways I needed to be pushed? She reminded me of home. But home can be too comfortable. After a certain age, you should move away from home. Right?

"Cassie makes me feel . . . I don't know . . . alive . . . nervous . . . energized. Cary, what do you think?"

"You'll just have to see what happens," he said.

I hated to be cynical, but I knew exactly what was going to happen when I found out my first one-on-one date was with Heather, who listed her occupation on *The Bachelor*'s official ABC website as "Never Been Kissed." Obviously the season had yet to air a single episode, but I had to believe by this time, five weeks and nearly a month and a half into production, there were people from her hometown of Carlsbad to Kathmandu who knew that Heather was going to have to find a new occupation before she left the show.

I might've been the only one with doubts. It wasn't about whether to kiss her as much as it was feeling right about being the one to take that from her, especially knowing I was more sold on other women. Finally, I decided my lips had a job to do. This wasn't about me—or my lips. It was about Heather. She'd signed up for the show. She wanted to have a good time. Why not give her a story to tell about her first kiss?

It was set up perfectly. We had a super-chill time sightseeing the Andaman coast in a Thai longboat. The night was warm, the tropical air soothing, and the setting seductive enough that we felt almost natural when we got up to stroll along the water and get into place where producers had told us to stand and talk and see what happens (as if they were getting their lines from Cary).

I'd been tipped off to the fact there was going to be a large fireworks display at a certain time and I should wait for them before kissing Heather, if that's what I felt like doing. As we waited, both of us were pulled for ITMs. While Heather was off doing her interview, one of the many stray dogs roaming the streets came up to me. When I bent down to pet him, he licked me on the lips. A few moments later, Heather returned, the fireworks exploded overhead, and I gave my second kiss of the night.

"I've kissed a boy and it felt so natural," Heather said later, pleased with the way things had gone and knowing, as I did, they weren't going any further.

Back at the hotel, the fireworks were just beginning. Elyse made a scene among the girls about not getting a one-on-one and then came to my room, where she complained about not having enough time with me to see if we really had a relationship. I didn't know whether she wanted to say "I do" or "goodbye"; she chose goodbye and walked off the show.

When no one begged her to come back, I have a feeling Elyse finally understood the show wasn't fake.

Our group date the next day involved a trip into the jungle, where we ate weird food, touched snakes and spiders and eels and other slimy, scary creatures us city folk typically see only on *National Geographic*'s Instagram page, and learned survival skills. The latter would've been nifty if they could've been applied to relationships, which were all over the place. Onyeka and Nicole Lopez-Alvar were going after each other; Tayshia was over it—or them; Sydney and Katie both wanted more time with me; Hannah B. confessed that she was falling in love with me, which I enjoyed hearing (who wouldn't), but it scared me.

As much as I liked Hannah B. and felt in some strange way like we'd already been through a lot, I also thought, dang, she got to the L-word barely knowing me. I wasn't ready to send her home yet, but I knew she wasn't the one. Neither were Caelynn and Tayshia, that much I was pretty certain. And Hannah G.?

That was the loop in my brain. It started to weigh on me in a way that hadn't happened until Hannah B. said she saw herself falling in love. That was a big holy-shit moment, where suddenly I felt the enormity and seriousness of holding people's hearts in my hand. It was a heavy responsibility.

Only one person didn't cause me to question or doubt myself, and I finally had a one-on-one date with her the next day. Cassie and I were going scuba diving. I wanted to hug my producers when they told me that I was getting my date with Cass. It had never been a case of her not being ready, they explained, as much as they wanted to save her for an adventure suited especially for her. Outdoors. Water. Swimming. I got it.

More than anything, I was thrilled about finally being with her where our time together wouldn't be cut short or interrupted. When I woke up early the next morning for my 8:00 a.m. predate interview and saw gray skies out the window, along with a slight drizzle, I worried they might postpone our date or change it to something boring indoors. They didn't, although there was a small modification.

Instead of scuba diving, we motored out to sea in a longboat until we got to a small sandbar. It was literally a teardrop of land sticking up slightly from the turquoise water. During the thirty-minute ride, I reminded Cass of how, after finding out we were going to Thailand, I'd raced over to the group of girls and announced all excited and goofy, "We're going to Thailand! Who's been to Thailand?" Both Cass and Caelynn had raised their hands, and the excitement just drained out of me.

"Oh man, you've been there, too?" I said. "Tough crowd."

Cassie patted my leg and gave me a sweet look before cooing, "Oh, I'm sorry." She had a story of her own. Every morning Chris Harrison and I and sometimes one of the executive producers ran a few miles up and down the beach, passing the private villa where the girls stayed each way. Cassie said they didn't know this until Chris mentioned it at dinner the other night. The next morning half of them were outside, waving and yelling good morning to us.

The best part of my date with Cassie, other than just being with her, was not having to worry about anyone waving or yelling or interrupting. On our private island, we were wonderfully, thrillingly, and very happily alone—that is if you didn't count our producers and the camera and sound guys. We didn't. As far as the two of us were concerned, we were by ourselves. For the nearly four hours, we played on the sandbar, talked, kissed, swam, and kissed some more, as if we truly were the only two people on the planet.

Half that time, though, was spent waiting for the rain to stop. Every half hour or so, it rained. And then it poured. Cass and I scrambled back onto the boat, in semi-shelter, but still getting drenched. I had my iPod with me, and we listened to country music and ate rice cakes. Both of us were Dan + Shay fans, and I had a ton of their music. We picked songs for each other: She played "All to Myself" for me, and I played "Speechless" for her.

About three-quarters of the way through, the sky cleared enough that the crew asked us to play around in the water while they took a cool drone shot from above. They didn't need any sound for the shot, so we took off our mics and dove in. While waiting for them to set up their shot, we splashed and talked, kissed and laughed, and that's when Cassie turned to me with a serious expression and asked the question that sliced through five weeks of production, ten thousand miles of travel, and thousands more kisses, tears, and minutes spent analyzing, thinking, worrying, and wondering: "How do you not know by now?"

Great question.

I'd been asking that same question or a variation of it practically all my life and never been able to answer it as definitively as I could at that moment. The irony was, I didn't tell Cass that I knew.

If I had, so many things that happened afterward might've been different. Now, with the perspective of time, I can see the consequences of abandoning the one tool I had for dealing with people that I knew was foolproof: honesty.

I wasn't dishonest with her. I just didn't come out and say, "I do know, and it's you." I wonder what would've happened if I had told her. But I couldn't. We were in the middle of a show. We still had six weeks to go. I couldn't blow the rest of the so-called competition. I had to be somewhat coy, which I explained.

But Cass wasn't asking out of curiosity. She had her reasons, starting with the obvious, "How did I not know?" She truly wanted to know. For her own peace of mind, she needed to know. She was an observer. She thought things through before stepping out or putting herself in an uncomfortable position. She knew other women were in the picture. She didn't want to be any more vulnerable than she already was.

I didn't know it, but she'd cried when I went on my one-on-one with Caelynn, who she actually liked as a friend.

How could I not know?

And if I did, why didn't I say it?

To be fair, I had not yet had my one-on-one with Hannah G. I had an out. I didn't know for sure. I was only 99.8 percent sure. I was grateful Cassie didn't press for an answer. Back on the boat, we snuggled against each other. With a light rain falling, we pulled the tarp over us, scrolled through songs, and talked about TV shows, movies, and favorite foods. We discovered that simple things like family, board games, and our pets made us the happiest.

"Don't get me wrong," Cass said. "This show is cool, and I'm obviously getting to do a bunch of great things. But I wish we could just go back to your place and hang out."

I gave her a wink, as if to say, "Just wait." I knew that dinner later on was at my place. The good times we were having together were going to continue. But not so fast. Back at the resort, as I finished my postdate interview and got dressed for dinner, I got word that Cassie was going to be late. It was delayed several more times before her producer, Brian Martinez—or Martini for short—came over and said dinner might have to be canceled. Cass wasn't feeling well.

My face registered the extreme disappointment I felt hearing this news. It wasn't just dinner that would have to be canceled. I'd persuaded producers to agree to give us some sexy time in my bedroom by ourselves after dinner. They knew how badly I wanted time with Cass. She'd been up for some additional alone time, too.

"It's a stomach thing," her producer explained. "She's been throwing up."

"Fuck it," I said, shrugging. "Please let her know that I'm sorry she's sick but I'm still kissing her."

A short time later I heard Cassie and her producer arrive at my door. Even though I knew she'd thrown up a few minutes before, I gave her a big kiss. We sat down at the table, beautifully set for a romantic dinner. The poor thing was shivering even though it was like 100 degrees outside. She'd planned to talk about how uneasy she felt with exposing so much of her private life on TV, but she was trying so hard to not throw up that she couldn't keep her thoughts straight. She ran out of the room several times mid-sentence and threw up.

After her last mad dash, she came back in with throw up in her hair and on her dress, gamely expecting to keep going or at least try. She wiped tears from her eyes. She was a freaking rock star, running out to yak and then coming back in to finish her story. We took a break, which helped. Cass returned and managed to eke out her concerns that some of her relatives would watch the show and think she didn't value herself the way she should after learning she wasn't a virgin and seeing her make out on TV.

I wanted to crack a joke, like would it help soften the blow that I was a virgin. But it wasn't the time or place. I also understood where she was coming from. Both of us were raised in families that emphasized conservative values, meaning we were to take things slow and respect our families as well as ourselves.

Cass got sick a couple more times before we got through the conversation. The second time she ran outside with one hand over her mouth while flashing me a peace sign behind her back with the other, like, *Keep the faith, I'll be right back*. It might be hard to imagine, but I thought that was so damn cute.

Even more adorable: when she came back inside, I said something like, "It's too bad this is happening. I had a nice night planned for us. My bedroom is right in there. I thought we could hang out."

Cass smiled meekly, stood up, and said, "Okay."

As she explained later, she'd been looking forward to this time together as much as I had and didn't want to give it up. We laid down on the bed and that seemed to help Cass. After a bit, she seemed to revive. We got under the sheets, not something you ordinarily see on the show, but I thought the extra layer of privacy might make Cass more comfortable given her fragile condition. It also created more intimacy. We relaxed. Soon I was telling her exactly how I felt about her. As the night went on, we were able to get a little more handsy than what might have happened if we'd been on top of the covers.

We laugh about it now.

It was love.

How did I know? How did we know?

Almost everything about the date had gone wrong, from the weather to Cassie's illness, and yet, at the end of the night and to this day, both of us would keep everything the same. Especially the one last touch that capped our time together: before she went back to her own room, Cassie got a rose.

PART FIVE

The First Time

Drama in Denver

Before leaving Thailand, we walked through a rose ceremony that felt more dutiful than any of those that had come before. Onyeka and Nicole were the two bachelorettes standing at the end without roses. We were going to Vietnam, and no one wanted to put up with their bickering anymore, especially not me.

I was getting a one-on-one date with Hannah G. Finally. Despite my feelings for Cassie, I knew spending time with Hannah G. was important. It was going to answer the tiny questions I had about the decision I would ultimately make. The time I had already spent with Hannah G. was enough to make me a huge fan and give me a sense that we could be very comfortable together. But it wasn't enough time to know whether there was anything more than being comfortable, which was the special ingredient I wanted in a relationship. I didn't want to wake up in the morning or go to sleep at night feeling comfortable. I wanted WOW.

For the daytime portion of our date, we went to a spa for massages, wraps, and pampering. Hannah arrived looking like a real-life Barbie doll in a red print dress. Any shorter and it would've been a shirt. "Every time I see her I get a little smitten," I said in my ITM, and I meant it. We held hands as we entered the spa, changed into swimsuits, and surrendered our bodies and inhibitions to a couples massage and body wraps on adjoining tables.

Seduced by our surroundings, we gravitated closer to each other until Hannah broke through the invisible barrier that separated us and rolled on top of me in her black bikini. After a mud bath, we showered together outdoors. The producers liked putting me in these situations where we pushed the limits of sexy. Not that I wasn't also a willing participant. I, too, liked promoting the fact that I could have these intimate moments and still save myself.

There was something I didn't consider until it happened: Those intimate moments included real physiological responses. They weren't on TV, but boners are a real, regular, and unavoidable part of the show. The producers are sensitive to guys who find themselves in a hard situation. I didn't know this until I was in the ocean with Cassie in Thailand and production said they needed me for an interview. I wasn't ready to get out of the water.

There was some confusion and shouting until one of the producers, picking up my efforts to discreetly communicate the issue, bought me more time. Poor Cass waited patiently while I splashed, yawned, swam, and waited for low tide.

Hannah G.'s black bikini had a similar effect on me. But I needed more of a reason for the two of us to be together. At dinner later that night, she told me about the difficulties she'd had as a kid when her parents divorced. I related my own experiences of seeing my family break apart. We definitely got along and had a good time. But once I was back at my villa and thinking about everything we'd talked about that day, I realized we never brought up what our life might be like together. The future didn't come up.

Was that significant? Or was I looking for excuses? Earlier, in my ITM, I'd told producers that I was falling in love with Hannah G., and in some way maybe I was. But as unsure as I was about Hannah G., I knew I was definitely falling in love with Cassie. It turned out she was thinking about me, too. She had feelings for me, too. But she wasn't close to being able to say I love you. She also felt like time was running out. She counted the number of girls left. She knew hometowns were around the corner. And then . . .

That frightened her. She wasn't *there* yet, and she wondered when or if she ever would be. Did a switch just flip one day? How would she know?

All through our group date, a day of martial arts training, we traded looks and smiles from afar. Without saying so, we pined for more time together. I complained to my producers. My poor, poor producers. I pity what they had to put up with from me, although I wasn't as concerned back then. I needed to vent.

Nancy urged me to keep my options open. "You never know what's going to happen. One of these girls might surprise you," she said.

I was done being surprised. I don't want to sound callous, but in just two months I'd learned that Hannah B. had been treated for anxiety and depression; Caelynn had been sexually assaulted; Elyse's sister had died of cancer; Heather had never been kissed; and Tayshia was ashamed of being divorced. More recently, Demi had revealed her mother was in federal prison. Not only did she tell me that, but while we were there in Vietnam, her mom was released and Demi asked me to be on the phone with her for their first call together.

It was heavy-duty—too heavy for some. Heather said she wasn't ready for me to meet her parents, and Sydney and Katie both complained they weren't getting enough time with me. So did Tayshia.

My second one-on-one date in this balmy destination was with Kirpa, who let me know she'd been engaged eight years to a guy who was adamant about staying a virgin until they tied the knot. They never did. Then Sydney flat-out said, "I need more," and left the show. How many had walked off so far?

There were times when I wanted to split, too. Before my date with Kirpa, there'd been a rain delay, and as we waited, someone in production let it slip that we were going to Denver when we finished in Vietnam. That picked me up from the funky mood I was in. I pictured home, my dog, my parents. It was going to be sweet.

Then I swung back the other way. At the outset, I'd asked producers to make sure no girls walked in on me while I was kissing another girl. Then, while I was kissing Demi—or while Demi was kissing me—Onyeka walked in, and I lost it. I ran off, pissed. Later, I saw it was less about that particular kiss and more that I started to feel guilty about kissing other women when what I told myself I needed was clarity on two, and what I knew I really wanted was to kiss only one of them, Cassie.

That night, Demi came to my room and said she was falling in love with me. I don't know if that was true. I think she intended to come over to have some fun and then go back to hang with the girls and stir the pot. That was her personality and there was much about her to appreciate. But I was finished playing games and sent her home soon after she left my room. At the rose ceremony, I also said goodbye to Katie, whose departure came with a warning to beware of fakers among the remaining girls.

It wasn't the first time I'd been cautioned that some of the girls might be thinking more about a post-show career than a relationship with me. But I knew these shots were fired in the heat of hurt feelings, which was unfortunate. I didn't waste energy worrying whether these things were true. I'd find out soon enough.

I flew to Denver independently of the girls and checked into a downtown hotel. They stayed nearby in an Airbnb mansion. Being back in familiar surroundings had a reenergizing effect on me. Being able to glance up at the Rockies was fuel for my soul. My schedule that week included three one-on-one dates, starting with Tayshia, who helped me walk Sniper, and impressed me as a smart, sensibile person. Over a tasty seafood dinner at the Denver Milk Market, I asked her about rumors of fakers in the house. She claimed to have overheard Cassie and Caelynn talking about becoming the next Bachelorette.

That was easily fact-checked. My next date was with Caelynn. I took her snowboarding and told her what Tayshia had said. Caelynn's reaction? A big, resounding F-bomb. She insisted that she and Cassie were being maligned and misunderstood. We ended up having a fine enough time together, but I had trouble getting past my anger at the girls who'd dragged Cassie's name into this drama. It had to be jealousy, and it just messed with my head. I knew Cassie wasn't leading me on or auditioning to become the Bachelorette.

She had a hard enough time revealing her personal life on this show. No way was she signing up for a second tour of duty.

Next, I went on a date with Hannah B. I took her to meet my parents. Suddenly the whole thing felt wrong and too rushed. I was also grumpy and off my game. Earlier, when I walked in to get Hannah, I came face-to-face with Cass. We locked eyes and my heart broke. I think hers did, too. Neither of us said a word, but I heard her voice inside my head, "How do you not know?" I did know.

I think Cass did, too. Once Hannah B. and I were safely out the door, Cassie dropped her brave façade and broke down and cried.

After that, I spent the rest of the day showing Hannah around Denver. We looked at houses, visited my parents, and went out to dinner—all the things I would've loved to do with Cassie, who stayed in my thoughts. Following dinner, I walked outside with Hannah and broke up with her. It was for the most honest of reasons. I didn't want to look her father in the eye in the next week's hometowns knowing we weren't going to end up together.

She was caught off guard and rightfully upset. "Just, like, listen to people," she said, before getting into her car. I nodded, seething inside, aware that I had to do something to make all this smack talk go away.

It all came to a head when I took Hannah G., Kirpa, Cassie, and Heather for a tour of the Rockies on the historic Georgetown Loop Railroad, the final part of this trip back home. The old steam engine train passed through some of the most beautiful scenery in the world and I barely saw any of it. I was supposed to ask who thought they deserved a hometown rose, but Heather had news for me: she was outta there. Another one not feeling it. I was fine with that. In my mind, I already knew who was going to the hometowns.

For my own peace of mind, though, I tried to get to the bottom of the rumors everyone had been talking about. Cassie broke down in tears—the first time she cried in front of me—and said people were twisting her words. "I wouldn't be here if I really, really didn't see something with you," she said. I hugged her tight and whispered, "It's okay. It's okay." Kirpa threw gas on the fire, saying she had "concerns" about Caelynn and Cassie. I thought, *Girl, you're lucky to be here these last three weeks. Chill.*

After the train ride, we changed clothes and reconvened for a fancy dinner. I sat opposite Hannah G., Cassie, and Kirpa. The train ride was long over, but this was really the end of the line for one of them. I only had two roses and less patience. I gave the first rose to Hannah G. without thinking of the effect it had on Cassie. It broke my heart to walk Hannah outside and see Cass left behind with Kirpa, wondering if I might be sending her home.

She could've stood up and said, "Make up your mind right now or I'm leaving," and I would've walked out with her. I probably should've done that. Imagine the promo that would've created. Anyway, before I sat back down, Caelynn snuck into the dinner to reassure me that Cass had no ulterior motives and I shouldn't have any doubts if the last rose was between her and Kirpa. "It's okay," I said. "I got this."

And I did. As I gave the last hometown rose to Cassie, I went off-script and told her that I was falling in love with her.

The truth was, I was already in love with her.

The truth was, I did know!

And her?

"I'm crazy for you," she responded.

It wasn't exactly the response I wanted to hear, and Cass knew that from the look on my face. But I focused on making sure she knew the way I felt about her and moved on. In recognition of the hard week I had had, the producers offered me a little more time with Cassie. I took her to the top of Union Station, one of Denver's most popular landmarks and a favorite spot of mine, where we drank champagne, enjoyed the view, and listened to country music. It was a thoughtful gesture among friends. We all recognized the occasional tension between us was unavoidable and also among the ingredients that made the show great.

Cass didn't want to leave, but at 4:00 a.m. I walked her to the elevator and rode down to the lobby with her. We couldn't keep our hands off each other. She had to catch an early morning flight back to LA and still had to pack. I told her I was looking forward to meeting her family before giving her one last kiss.

I watched her walk outside, get in a waiting car, and drive off. As the car disappeared from sight and I tried to picture meeting up with her again on the beach in her hometown, I thought, *she has to know, too.*

The Game Changer

I t was midway through the hometowns, and Tayshia and I were standing in the back of a plane, looking down at the world through an open door from an altitude of about thirteen thousand feet. I thought I was going to die. But what the hell, right? I said to myself, "If I die, this will have been one helluva ride." Then I leaned close to my instructor, Mike, who was about five and a half feet tall and 130 pounds, and shouted, "Let's do it!" It was the perfect metaphor for the entire week of hometowns. I survived.

CAN I HAVE YOUR BLESSING TO MARRY YOUR DAUGHTER #1

The week began in Fredericksburg, Virginia, where I met up with Caelynn. For the sake of being respectful to the families and the premise of the show, I agreed to ask each girl's father for permission to get engaged to his daughter, starting with Caelynn's stepfather. I lied when he asked if I saw a future with his daughter. Her mom sensed as much when she said, "I don't know if you're ready. I don't know if Caelynn's ready." I think she correctly pegged both of us. Caelynn's sister had the same skeptical vibe, but it might've been that they knew Caelynn wasn't ready to say "I do" to anyone, not just me. Finally, I asked her stepdad for permission. He responded with a question. It was a tie, and the tie goes to the runner, and . . .

Actual response: "Are you ready, truly, to get married?"

What he really meant: You might be ready, but there's no way in hell she's ready.

Takeaway: I am so relieved to be getting out of here.

CAN I HAVE YOUR BLESSING TO MARRY YOUR DAUGHTER #2

I was off to Birmingham, Alabama, where Hannah G. grew up. As a warm-up, we took an etiquette class that served as both primer and warning to me that courtships were done a little different in the South than they were on TV. Hannah's parents were lovely people, and their home was a reflection of them as solid, family-oriented folks. I could tell I didn't fit in, and that probably wouldn't disappoint her parents. "You've known each other for, what, a month now?" her dad said. I still asked him for his blessing, as I did with each girl's father. "Let's not rush anything," he said in a tone that I appreciated. "Let's see what happens."

Actual response: "If it continues working the way it is, I'd give you my blessing for sure."

What he really meant: Yeah, man, do whatever you want to do. Just get these cameras out of my house.

Takeaway: I don't know where this is going with your daughter, but you and I should play golf together sometime.

NOBODY PUTS BABY IN THE CORNER

When I returned to my hotel, Hannah B. was waiting in the lobby. "You're in my hometown," she said. Seeing her was not a total surprise, and I took her up to my room. She was still stewing about not getting a rose and wanted more clarity from me. In reality, it seemed she wanted to lash out and vent. She went off on the remaining four girls and told me they didn't have the qualities that made her so amazing. It was the beast in her, roaring and raging. I put my hand up, signaling her to stop. "Hannah, I don't know what you want me to do," I said. "I don't have the energy to put into this conversation. I'm not in a relationship with you anymore. Period."

Actual response: "You're never going to find what I got."

What she really meant: You better not pick Caelynn.

Takeaway: It's fine if you want to talk, but next time I'm going to put the game on and turn up the volume.

CAN I HAVE YOUR BLESSING TO MARRY YOUR DAUGHTER #3

I met with Tayshia's family at their home in Santa Ana, California. As soon as I met them, I was reminded of the hesitations I had about hometowns. They involved families with complex dynamics and people who hadn't signed up for this *Bachelor* craziness. I'd seen the reservations in my own family. They wanted to do a good job for me but would have passed if the decision had been solely up to them. Tayshia's family seemed to feel similarly. They were reluctant voyagers. "You don't microwave relationships," her dad told her. I couldn't have agreed more, even as I asked his permission to marry his daughter.

Actual response: "Colton! Wow. Man, you're laying it on me. I appreciate you laying it out. But I just met you."

What he really meant: You can't microwave a relationship.

Takeaway: What he said.

CAN I HAVE YOUR BLESSING TO MARRY YOUR DAUGHTER #4

I knew Cassie was extremely close to her family, which made me all the more excited to finally meet them at their home in Huntington Beach, California. This was a house where I wanted to fit in before I even arrived. We met up at the beach for a surfing lesson, her way of introducing me to her beachside hometown. Her blond, surfer-girl good looks aside, Cassie was really skilled at riding waves. Her younger brother, Landon, then seventeen and an aspiring pro surfer, joined us in the water, along with several of his buddies. He paddled up to me and said, "Dude, this is so crazy. How are you doing all this?"

One at a time.

I was literally shaking outside her house a few hours later. Cassie reviewed the names of everyone waiting inside—her dad, Matt; her mom, Amy; her sister, Michelle; her brother, Landon; her brother's girlfriend, Saige; and her two aunts, Sandy and Annie. She warned they were going to be very protective. A few months before *The Bachelor*, they'd nursed her through a difficult breakup and were wary of a repeat performance. They were waiting for us in the she was special. He gave me the clear sense that he didn't want Cassie getting engaged at the end of the show. Like the other fathers I'd spoken to, he didn't think we'd spent much time together, certainly not enough to take a forever step like marriage, and he was right again. What he did give me was permission to keep dating his daughter, if that's what she wanted.

The thing was, I agreed with him on every point—Cass and I barely knew each other, and yes, as inopportune as it was, there were those other girls. I would've said the same thing had I been in his same position. Our values and beliefs were very much in line with each other. The part that hurt me was hearing that when asked his impression of me, he'd said, "You know, he's a guy." I didn't see myself as just another guy, another typical guy.

I'd spent my entire life working to be outstanding in every way I knew how, and I wished he could see that I would be outstanding for his daughter, too.

Actual response: "Marriage is a lifelong commitment. That's big and shouldn't be taken at all lightly, because it is forever, in my opinion. Too often, I think, it's done without enough thought. So I feel, as far as the hand in marriage, that would be a premature blessing."

What he really meant: Get out of my house and take my daughter on another date, dude.

Takeaway: Not a fan of *The Bachelor*.

I tried to brush it off, but Matt's response was a lot to process. I was pissed and frustrated. Not at him or what he said; frankly, I agreed with him. We hadn't spent much time together. How many weeks had it been in total? And how much time within each of those weeks had we spent together? Not much. Not enough in terms of

third-floor living room, and I was literally blinded when I enter
everybody was blond and gorgeous.

I picked out Cassie's sister, Michelle, and Landon's girlfrier
but I had no idea which one of the remaining blond women w
her mom. I held out the flowers and said, "This is for Mom." Thai
goodness Amy stepped forward and said, "That's me." Cassie s
between me and her dad. Her right hand was wrapped aroun
mine, and her left hand held on to her father's hand. That sai
everything I needed to know about the challenges ahead of me.

Their dinnertime reminded me of my own family. They put th
food on the kitchen counter and then everyone stood around, eating and talking. In the meantime, producers began pulling people
in combinations for interviews. Cassie was asked to steal her dad
for a few minutes, while I went to another room to talk with Cass's
mom. Cassie's aunts turned out to be fans of the show.

"How do you think you're doing?" Annie asked.

"Have you ever made Cassie the last rose?" Sandy inquired.

I thought the night was going well until I got with Cassie's
dad. We went outside and sat in two chairs next to their fire pit.
A successful marketing executive who ran his own business, Matt
was strong, principled, and deeply protective of his children. Matt
had probably spent the last ten years chasing boys away from the
house, so as far as he was concerned, I was a problem before I
walked through the front door.

That didn't stop me from telling him how special I thought Cass
was and how much she meant to me. He appreciated my words but
was rightfully skeptical given that I had spent the week asking three
other fathers for permission to marry their daughters. He was like
yeah, yeah, but you have three other girls, and you know what? He
had a point.

I argued that Cassie was different. Obviously, he already knew planning a lifetime together. I looked at Cass, feeling so grateful I had met her and wishing . . . well, obviously I wished we'd spent more time together. I also wished I had slightly different answers for her parents.

I really liked her family. We had some great conversations.

I didn't even think about telling her that her dad hadn't given me permission. Probably because I hadn't wanted to ask the question in the first place. I knew it was stupid.

What I wanted to know was how she felt about me. The previous week I'd told her that I was falling for her. Now I wanted to hear how she was feeling about me.

"I want to be one hundred percent confident in anything I say to you," she said. "I don't want to say something that I don't fully know. I know I don't want this to be over."

I wondered how we went from *I'm falling in love with you* to *I don't want this to be over*. What was I missing? With the night over and the four hometowns completed, I got into the black SUV waiting for me and saw my producer, Eileen, hiding in the back, out of camera range. She asked how I was doing. I told her the truth: not good.

"What's going on?"

"Too much shit has gone down. I'm tired of it. I don't want to do this anymore."

Fantasy Versus Reality

Portugal was next. And fantasy suites.

But everything was messed up. The ride back to the hotel was painful. I said goodnight to Eileen and sat in my room, in the dark, feeling alone and confused. I was completely in love with Cass and wanted to figure out what to do, now more than ever. Except it wasn't just up to me. I needed to hear where she was at. Clearly. And for real. As she had an hour or so earlier when she'd said she was falling in love with me. Then, somehow, we'd slid backward, and now I sensed she might be thinking about breaking up with me.

Cassie is the Queen of I Don't Know, and she really didn't know what to do. She went out with her producer and spent the whole time asking him for advice. The hometown had confused her. How could she move forward without the full, unconditional support of her family? Did she need to leave the show before flying all the way to Europe? Or should she end things in Portugal? Suddenly, she wondered the same thing as her parents: What was the point when I was still dating other girls? Or did she want to go? Was she falling in love with me? Was there a chance I was the guy for her?

I remember flying to Portugal and thinking about Cassie and her family throughout the entire thirteen-hour flight. I didn't need to watch any movies or read a book. Every moment I'd spent with her replayed itself in my head. All I wanted to do was sit and talk with her and hang out more with her family, minus the cameras and the coaching. I realized I had a chance to spend this kind of previous alone time with Cassie in the fantasy suites—that is, if she didn't break up with me first, which was my biggest fear.

We just needed more time together. Alone.

After a long flight to Portugal, I checked into an intimate luxury hotel near the seaside town of Algarve. The next day I worked with the crew on B-roll, shooting all around the city. Whatever happened with me and Cass, I was appreciative of the ways the show was broadening my life's experiences. First Asia and now Europe—the travel was blowing my mind. So was the challenge ahead of me.

The original list of thirty girls was down to three—Hannah G., Cassie, and Tayshia. Back in LA, at the rose ceremony that followed hometowns, I sent Caelynn home. Under different circumstances, I would've cut Tayshia, but I wanted to separate Cassie and Caelynn. I knew their friendship had grown and thought it might be interfering with my relationship with Cass. If Caelynn went home, it might let Cassie see that I was more serious about her.

My overnights with these women were scheduled to start the next day, beginning with Tayshia followed by Cassie and Hannah G. A typical guy would have thought all of his dreams had come true. But as the world would see soon enough, I wasn't typical. I was deeply smitten with one girl in particular, and the only overnight I wanted was with her.

On my way to dinner that night, I saw several producers in the hotel dining room. I needed to talk to them if only for my own mental health. I sat down and let them know I'd thought about Cassie the whole flight over to Portugal and was still thinking about her—and only her. "I don't want to do this anymore," I said. "I can't fake it." They knew me well and listened to me vent until I simply ran out of gas and went back to my room for some much-needed sleep.

The next morning Tayshia and I got together. We went on a helicopter tour of the coast and picnicked along the water. I had a tough time with all the little things that made the date feel authentic. I didn't want to be there. In fact, mentally, I was already elsewhere. I was thinking about Cassie and spending the next day with her.

Tayshia had no idea any of this was going on when we met for dinner later that night. She opened up about being a virgin when she got married and the pain of discovering her husband had cheated on her. Then we went back to the fantasy suite and, as viewers saw, I opened a bottle of champagne and poured two glasses. By two or three in the morning, Tayshia realized that nothing was going to happen. Picking up on my vibe—or lack of one— she asked how I could be into her when she was so different from Cassie and Hannah G.

"Eh, don't worry about it," I said, closing the door on any further discussion. Tayshia soon fell asleep on half of the bed, and eventually I laid down next to her in my sweatpants and long-sleeved shirt. I didn't sleep all night.

In the morning, we got breakfast and I told the gaggle of producers who met with us that I didn't sleep all night and didn't want to do any of the interviews or B-roll planned for later in the day. I wanted to catch up on my sleep before my day with Cassie, if that happened. I said "if" based on a hunch, a sense I had that disaster was on its way. Like the smell of an approaching storm, it was in the air.

A full day of rest did nothing to quell my paranoia that Cass was breaking up with me. My pre-interview with producers supported that suspicion. After doing countless interviews the past couple of months, I was able to use the tenor of the questions as a barometer of what was going to happen later. I thought Nancy's questions were preparing me for disappointment, to the degree that I worried Cassie might not even show up.

But there she was, later that morning, walking toward me, and a moment later we embraced. She looked as happy and eager to see me as I was to spend time with her again. It was as if nothing was wrong, as if I'd imagined everything from the past week. We drove to Tavira, a tiny romantic town on the coast, and strolled along the quaint streets. We shopped and ate lunch as if we didn't have anything else to do. The tenor of the afternoon changed when we found a place to sit and review her hometown. Cass said she still had a lot to figure out.

She made it clear that her father's opinion was extremely important to her. I explained it was important to me, too. I wanted her to understand that I wasn't going to get down on one knee, especially on TV, without everyone in her family being on board, especially her dad, which wasn't likely to happen anytime soon. "I only hoped I might end up with someone as great as you," I said. "As far as I'm concerned, this is an obstacle, not the end. What else can I say or do?"

Cassie ran her fingers through her hair, unleashing her blond locks so that her face all but disappeared. When she re-emerged, her eyes were full of tears, poised to overflow. "I just thought he'd trust me and support me," she said.

We didn't resolve anything before producers pulled us to do our mid-date interviews. Which was frustrating. I wanted to be with Cassie, period. The more I talked about it, the more emphatic I grew. Before the interview ended, I flat-out said that I loved her. There it was, stated in the open, and I felt good about it. As I walked to my car, I glimpsed Cass still doing her interview, and she was crying. I knew her tears were not a good sign.

Flipping the Cheese Board

As I got ready for our dinner, I was excited, nervous, and extremely anxious. Only one thing was on my mind: getting on the same page as Cass. I might've been way too optimistic or hopeful or just misreading her, but I felt like we weren't far apart and hoped we could reach an understanding by the end of the night.

Then she arrived for dinner and my heart dropped. I knew something was off. It was in her eyes, and it scared me.

We sat uneasily next to each other on a sofa while cameras adjusted around us. There was a cheese board and a bottle of wine on the table in front of us. I made a toast and then asked Cass if she wanted to make one. She said no. I realized small talk was out and we needed to get right into addressing our relationship and whether we were going to have one when this dinner was finished.

"My dad actually showed up at my hotel room," Cass said, looking up timidly for my reaction.

That was the first time I heard that Matt had shown up at the hotel after our lunchtime date. Cassie was surprised but grateful to see him. She was wracked with confusion, and Matt gave her the extra strength, support, and confidence she needed to figure out what she wanted to do. He said she shouldn't make a decision unless she was completely sure—and obviously she wasn't. He didn't want her to cave to the pressure and said she'd know when she was in love without having a single doubt, as was the case with him and her mom.

It was all clear and perfect and everything a parent should do. I'm sure that's why my old pal, supervising producer Ruby Taylor, had called Matt in the first place. She'd contacted him several days earlier and told him that Cassie was really struggling with her feelings and could use him as a sounding board.

Matt had dropped everything and flown almost halfway around the world to support his daughter. I wasn't surprised. He was that kind of father, the kind of dad I hoped to be someday—present for my child, putting family first. But it made me feel like production was working against me and trying to help Cassie break up with me. Why weren't they fighting for our relationship? Was the season supposed to end with a broken heart? Or was it supposed to end in a happily ever after love story?

Maybe it was my fault. Maybe I had led everyone to believe that I wanted to be with Hannah G. She was indeed my top choice for a long time. But from Thailand on I made it clear that I was in love with Cassie. Maybe I wasn't clear enough.

Did it matter? The second Cassie said her dad had traveled all the way to Portugal to speak with her, I knew I'd lost her.

Our conversation was raw. Much of what we said to each other was on the episode when it aired in March. I did my best to explain the way I felt and address her doubts, as if through sheer passion and force of will I could bring her around and convince her to say the words I wanted to hear. I apologized for what she went through in Denver and said I knew we needed more time together. If I'd been able to, I would've spent the whole time with her.

Suddenly I could no longer control myself. Words failed, emotions exploded, and I picked up the cheese board in front of us and threw it across the floor. Cassie and I laugh about it now and even make fun of it. If I get angry, Cass will yell, "Cheese board!" But back then there was nothing funny about it. "I love you," I said, my voice choking with emotion. "I want to be with you. I don't want to be with anybody else."

At that moment, only one thing mattered to me: saving my relationship with Cassie. I told her that I didn't care about getting engaged at the end of the season. I didn't care about the show anymore, either. If she needed more time to get to know me, I wanted to give her that time. Whatever amount of time she needed. I didn't know how to be any clearer: She might be ready to walk out, but I wasn't done fighting for us. And if she did leave, I was done being the Bachelor. There would be no point.

It was too much for the Queen of I Don't Know. She called a time out, got up, and took a brief stroll to gather her thoughts. She looked to her producer for support and guidance, but the decision was hers. It was too much for her. She hit circuit overload, to the point where the easiest thing for her to do was also the hardest thing: walk away.

When we sat down again and resumed our conversation, she famously said, "Today was perfect, and I love you so much . . . I couldn't . . . after today, I'm not, like, in love."

Those words went straight through me.

I'm not, like, in love.

I wondered if her mind had been made up the entire time.

"Did you tell your dad you were leaving tonight?" I asked.

She nodded. "Yes."

"Okay, then you're leaving tonight," I said.

I was unable to say anything else. I was in shock. My head was a storm of thoughts blowing through a dark sky.

"I'm not going to stop fighting for you," I said.

Cassie didn't want me to stop. Neither was she ready to quit herself. What she wanted and needed was to get the hell out of there to save herself. She was exhausted, confused, and simply overwhelmed—by the show, the events in the days and weeks leading up to this point, the buildup of emotion, the conflicting emotions, the talks with her producer, and everything I was telling her.

She was burned out and unsure of who to trust other than her dad. As she later told me, she needed to leave in order to breathe again. It was like she needed to run out of the burning house before she suffocated. There was no more oxygen. Maybe then she could figure out how she really felt and what she should do. Only many months later, after Cass and I spoke, did I fully understand her position.

As she said, I knew what was going on with the relationships I had with the other girls and everything going on behind the scenes. She was completely in the dark. She didn't know who to trust, including me. How could she trust me when I was still in relationships with two other girls? How could she let herself fall in love when she didn't trust the situation? How could she be in love with someone she couldn't trust?

She was at the point where she didn't even trust herself. Hence the importance of her dad jetting to her side. All Cass knew for sure was that she wasn't ready to get engaged. Not to me. Not to anybody. And Matt gave her the wherewithal to stand up for what was best for her—and that was to go home.

I walked Cassie out to her van and said goodbye. Our last words to each other were "I love you."

Then I went to my cabin. By the time I got there, I knew I had to do the same thing as Cass. Get the hell out of there.

I ran up the stairs, unzipped my bag, grabbed my wallet, put it in my back pocket, and headed back outside. I opened the door and saw a camera pointed at me. If I regretted anything from that night, it was hitting the camera. It wasn't my property. But I slapped it out of the way, out of my face, ripped off my microphone, and headed for the gate.

Outta Here

I saw the front gate and knew where I had to go. Up and over. I never considered the height of the gate or whether I could pull myself up and hurdle to the other side. I just did it. I expected to get caught the moment my feet touched the ground on the other side. When that didn't happen, my adrenaline kicked in and I started to run through the Portugal wilderness.

I had no idea where I was or where to go. In a white shirt, jeans, and Chelsea boots, I was not exactly dressed for a breakout and a long run, either. The road was empty and dark. I picked a direction, took off, and kept a good pace for what seemed like two miles.

I saw lights up ahead and ran toward them while making a plan. I was going to find the US embassy, use the documents in my wallet to get a temporary passport, and fly home. I'd pay for it myself. I never considered there might not be a US embassy in the small town where I was headed (there wasn't). Or a bank. Or a taxi. Or anything else that might get me from Portugal to Denver before the show's producers caught me.

I just wanted to go home and be done with *The Bachelor*.

I heard people calling my name in the distance. "He is gone," Chris Harrison said, which I saw on YouTube months later, and which was also true. I was gone; swallowed by the darkness. Three

or four vehicles drove by looking for me. Each time I ran up someone's driveway and hid behind a car. Or I darted into the woods.
I was surprised I didn't get shot or attacked by some animal. I
remember hearing a growl while I was hiding in someone's backyard and bracing myself to get jumped by a large dog.

I felt safer back in the middle of the road. Fairly soon after I
quit hiding, an SUV caught up with me. I heard Chris yelling my
name. I ignored him and kept walking. This went on for a bit. I saw
a light bouncing against the darkness beyond me and assumed I
was being videotaped. When I finally turned around, I looked at the
camera guy and said, "I hope you have a few extra battery packs
because it's going to be a long walk for you."

Chris shouted at me: "Where are you going, dude?"

"I'm going somewhere," I said. "I'm getting away from y'all."

"Come on, Colton. We're in the middle of nowhere."

"Y'all can call Jason or Blake and film a new season."

I wanted them to know how angry I really was. Once I felt
confident they got the message, I needed a graceful way out of this
situation. I was too tired to keep walking down this dark road. By
this time, other producers had pulled up and parked alongside the
road. It was 2:30 a.m., and I'd been out there for more than an
hour when the show's top producers and I huddled and had the
most impromptu production meeting in the show's history.

I heard phones buzzing with text messages. The sounds of a
crazy night: crickets, barking dogs, and buzzing phones. I didn't
know whether to laugh, scream, cry, put my hands up in surrender,
or what. I had a feeling no one else knew what to do, either. It was
6:30 p.m. back in Los Angeles. Everyone at the network would
know I'd gone AWOL. I could only imagine what those messages
said.

He jumped the fence.

How tall is the fence?

WTF?!?!?!

We found him.

He's pissed.

He's crazy.

He says he has a plan.

"Here's what I want to do," I said, slowly, clearly, and with growing assurance that my vision was correct. "I want to break up with the other two girls. Obviously I had my Fantasy Suite date with Tayshia, who is great, but I wasn't into it and just wanted to get through it. I don't want to put Hannah through that same thing. I want to break up with her, too. She's not going to understand. I didn't even give her a chance. But I have to do it. Then I want to talk to Cass and tell her that she's the only one."

I turned around and walked to one of the cars.

The texts continued to fly. I could only imagine them.

He's coming back.

What's he want to do?

He wants to break up with them.

What?

He's in the car.

With Tayshia and Hannah.

They're with him?

No, he wants to break up with them.

WTF?!?!?!

He's still into Cassie.

Copy that.

Telling Cass

It was 3:30 a.m. when I returned to the hotel and continued talking with producers about what to do next. Everyone was happy to be back in a comfortable hotel room and not standing on the side of the road. Several high-ranking producers who hadn't been outside joined us. For their benefit, I repeated my plan to break up with Tayshia and Hannah and then sit down with Cassie if she was up to it.

My goal was to get in front of her, I said, and let her know that she was the one and only one, and hopefully get the two of us moving forward again. Baby steps would be fine with me. I had no problem if they wanted to tape part of all of that; it was fine with me.

The room was quiet when I finished. *The Bachelor* brain trust digested the details and shared a few thoughts among themselves. Their ability to think quickly and actually produce on the fly was impressive. "Cassie's dad is still here," one of the lead producers said. "We can keep them if you want to talk to him again. And you can definitely talk with the other two and break up with them. We have a lot to figure out and plan and adjust. Then you can talk to Cass—that is, if she wants to. We won't force her."

"Sounds good to me," I said. "I'll take my chances."

Nancy woke me up later that morning and the day was a blur.

I went to wardrobe and told Cary everything while I got dressed. "I swear to God, I didn't think that was going to happen," he said. "You told me that you sensed she was going to break up with you. I can't believe it." Then came a sit-down with Chris Harrison, which was essential. Viewers would need to know what had happened— and why. I'd been sprinting down a dark road at 2:00 a.m. the last time I saw Chris. He walked in eager to see how I was doing after several hours of sleep. He was concerned. He was also Chris, letting me know that the previous night had been pretty weird.

Once the cameras went live, I told him everything. The show's editors could figure out how to make sense of it, but I described the boiling point I'd reached the night before and explained why I wasn't ending up with Hannah G., as everyone thought. The reason was simple and maybe even obvious to those watching with an outsider's perspective. I couldn't stop thinking about Cassie. I wanted to have a relationship with her and I was willing and ready to follow her back to Huntington Beach and start over.

"You can't help who you fall in love with," I said. "I love her."

"But she didn't give you that in return," Chris said.

"I don't believe it," I said, shaking my head in disagreement. "I'm in this relationship. I feel like something was off. Like something was holding her back."

"What are your next steps?"

"I am going to break up with Tayshia and Hannah."

And that's what happened. My first stop was Tayshia's hotel suite. Right before seeing her, I took a breath, feeling like an eternity had passed since our date, and then once we were face-to-face I knew it was the right thing to do. Our talk was civilized and straightforward and honest. I'm pretty sure she could tell this wasn't contrived or planned, and it confirmed what she already knew from our night together.

My conversation with Hannah was harder. She didn't have any idea why I wanted to meet with her, and in the aftermath of our wonderful, intimate date in Vietnam, she had every reason to believe that I wanted to give her a ring. Had I done that, I believe she was ready to say yes.

I felt terrible as I knocked on her hotel room door. No one wants to be the bearer of bad news of hurt another person's feelings, especially someone with whom you have a personal connection the way we did. Hannah was journaling when she let me in. She greeted me with a smile and a hug, totally unsuspecting and open and expectant of something good. Then I watched as all that changed—first into an expression of shock and then tears, vulnerability, and hurt. She said I didn't give her a chance.

This wasn't about giving her a chance. It was about my chance with Cassie. My chance at convincing someone else to give me a chance. It was all confusing, on the very edge of being too much to handle or figure out, and at stake was everything; and that's what I had my own mini breakdown as I left Hannah's room. "What the hell am I doing?" I said to no one in particular. "What the hell is going on?"

In the meantime, Cass and her dad were hanging out together. Some of that was filmed, but there came a point where they were off mic and her dad asked if she wanted to go for a walk. They snuck off together and had a long talk where they ran through hypotheticals.

Ironically, I later learned that Matt asked, "What if he breaks up with the other two and he comes back for you?"

Cass said, "That would be cool, huh?"

The walk turned out to be therapeutic for Cass. Confused, struggling, and overwhelmed, she was able to vent and at least try to figure things out. Only she could determine how she felt. She still didn't know that I'd jumped the wall, broken up with Tayshia and

Hannah, and planned to talk to her. But in a sign that the two of us were still on the same wavelength, though neither of us knew what the other was doing, she let herself think that maybe she wasn't finished yet. As she and her dad returned to their hotel, she admitted, "This is much harder than I thought it would be. I don't know what I want to do."

I was also sorting through my thoughts. My favorite producer, Eileen, came to my room with a camera operator and a sound man, Rocky and T. J. We talked for two hours. In my opinion, it was the best interview I did all season. We covered everything, from jumping the fence to my feelings for Cassie to my thoughts on family and the desire we all have to make a life that's meaningful and filled with love.

Rocky was in tears as we finished. He put his camera down and gave me a hug. "Dude, I get it," he said. "I'm in my forties, and I probably wouldn't have done what you did. But you're in your twenties. That's when you take risks. You take chances. You lead with your heart. Only you can know if what you did is right for you, but hey, it makes sense to me. I'm proud of you. I'm rooting for you."

My night was restless. I didn't know what was going to happen with Cass, how she was going to react, and if she even wanted to see me. For all I knew, she had packed and was leaving on an early morning flight. I only knew I had to risk it all to get it all.

The next morning, I was driven to Cassie's hotel. We talked nervously about whether there would be a show without a clear ending. The crew didn't know if they were advancing to the next location, Mallorca. It was up to me—and more so, Cass. Then came the moment when all would be decided. We parked near her hotel room and I got out of the car. She still didn't know I was there. I took a deep breath as I walked to her door and knocked.

As soon as she opened the door and saw it was me on the other side, she smiled. I thought, okay, that's a good start. At least her dad hadn't answered the door! "I missed you," we both said. I gave her a big hug and asked if we could talk. We grabbed each other's hands, got in the elevator, and hugged the whole ride down.

"I'm glad you're here," she said.

"I'm glad that I'm here, too," I said.

Once we got to the quiet spot that had been prepped for our talk, I explained that I'd broken up with Tayshia and Hannah and wanted to be in a relationship with her. She was shocked. After two and a half months of always having at least an idea of what to expect in a one-on-one conversation, she was completely and utterly surprised. I remember Cass even laughed a tiny bit when I said, "Yeah, the other two went home." But she quickly caught herself, blaming her reaction on the shock of it all.

"That's not funny," she said. "I just can't believe it."

She had a hard time processing it.

"You really did that? For us?"

"Yeah, one hundred percent."

I went on and made sure Cass understood that moving forward with her in a relationship was more important to me than getting engaged for the sake of the show. There'd be no more talk of a proposal or marriage. I knew the show's premise and it didn't matter anymore. As far as I was concerned, the goal was for Cass and me to get to know each other. We'd figure it out together. Day by day. The only thing I wanted from her was a second chance.

I saw the relief in her eyes.

There wasn't going to be any more talk of forever. I was only asking for today and hopefully tomorrow. Though still nervous and uncertain, that was a time frame Cass could handle. I said my family was in Spain, waiting to meet her, and I hoped she'd go there with me. She said yes. Everyone around us had a grin on their face.

I had to make sure of one more smile. I met Cassie's dad in a small café area at the hotel. Cass had gasped, "Oh my God," when I told her that I wanted to speak with her dad. She had a few minutes to speak with him before I got to him. But the job of bringing him up to speed essentially fell on my shoulders. I told him everything, and his reaction to the breakups and slower pace I described was much more positive.

We actually joked about asking for his blessing again, but there was no need. I knew where he stood. He knew the way I felt, too. Most important, Cassie had let both of us know how she felt. For the first time, we were all in agreement.

We were all good.

And I hoped we really were.

An Invitation

Mallorca, Spain. A beautiful estate with flowers everywhere. I walked in and saw my family, gave them big hugs, and told them how comforting it was to see all of them after some very emotional, draining last few days. I filled them in, not knowing how they'd react but assuming they'd be relieved they only had to meet one girl, not two as would've been the case if things had followed the traditional plan. My dad said, "This was the best thing you could've done for us. Having more than one girl would've been a weird situation."

I nodded. "Tell me about it."

After I prepped them, they had concerns about meeting a girl who'd already broken up with me. But they were ready to help figure out where Cassie's head was at and provide any insights they gleaned from talking to her.

"We'll try to get to the bottom of it," my mom said.

I went outside to get Cassie and escort her to the patio where my family would be waiting for her. I walked up to her idling van and was told she wasn't ready to come out. Something was off. I could tell. Then the door finally slid open and my fears were confirmed. I could see she was upset and had been crying. Her eyes met mine and they were filled with fear. I said to myself, "Oh shit, she's about to break up with me again."

It turned out Cassie had been having a panic attack inside the van. She'd freaked herself out: What if my parents didn't like her? What if the entire family didn't like her? We walked to a nearby bench, sat down, and I listened. For whatever reason, she chose that moment to open up about her ex and how that relationship had made her feel controlled and manipulated and, as she said, "I know you aren't in any way like that. But I don't know. Maybe I've got some PTSD right now."

So many revelations. I understood more about Cassie right there than I had the entire time. I told her to take a breath. There was no pressure. All she had to do was be herself. My family was going to love her.

And they did. Everyone in my family played their roles, and Cassie felt much better by the end. Then producers took us back to our separate hotels to rest and regroup. The next day, Cassie and I met up again and went on an outdoor adventure. They had us rappel down a rocky cliff with picturesque views of the island to one side and the ocean for as far as we could see. Both of us appreciated the workout along with the related message of trusting your partner as you go up and down life's uncharted paths.

Afterward, we went back to our respective hotels again, until later that night, when we met up again for a romantic dinner. This was the big one, our date prior to spending the night together in the fantasy suite, if she accepted my invitation. This was our redo, the date we didn't get to have in Portugal, and I couldn't have been happier with the way things worked out as soon as I saw Cassie again. As she walked across the bridge to meet me, she was smiling, her eyes were dancing, and she was glowing with happiness.

Conversation at dinner was mostly light and breezy, which both of us welcomed, given all the heavy discussions we'd had the past couple of days. But one heavy topic arose when Cass asked why I hadn't told anyone other than Caelynn about my previous relationship. Apparently Caelynn had come back from our dinner in Singapore and told some of the other girls that I'd opened up to her about Aly, which showed the trust I had in her. It was bullshit, and I told Cass everything. Given what was ahead of us, it let me explain why I took relationships and sexual intimacy as seriously as I did. It involved fear and pain.

"The show helped me address some of those issues," I said. "But I still have to learn how to enjoy it."

Cass was glad I felt comfortable opening up to her about something that made me feel vulnerable.

"I'm fine being patient," Cass said. "I want to take things slow."

She put her hand on top of mine, and through that tiny gesture I felt the strength of this very special woman. I sensed the true beginning of what I hoped would be a lifelong quest of discovering and appreciating her uniqueness as a friend, a lover, and a human being. I hoped and prayed I could make her feel the same way.

"I'm glad last week went the way it did," she said. "Even though it was hard, I think we both needed it."

A perfect segue to dessert. I lifted up my place mat and revealed an envelope: the invitation for our fantasy suite. " 'Colton and Cassie, welcome to Mallorca, Spain. Should you choose to forgo your individual rooms, please use this key to stay as a couple in the fantasy suite. Chris Harrison.' "

Before I could ask, Cass already had the key in her hand.

We got to the fantasy suite and inside, we found it stocked with champagne and desserts. It was funny because, for the cameras, they'd had the doors open for a while and we found a really fat ginger cat who'd made herself comfortable there. A cat lover, Cassie cooed that it was so fluffy and pretty and we should leave her be. But there was no way I was sleeping with this stray cat in our room. It was our first domestic dust-up. In the end, we chased it out, and then we chased out all the producers and crew members.

After the last person left and the door closed, Cass and I sat down together and took like the biggest deep breaths of our lives. Both of us were relieved to be unmic'd and not staring into a camera sharing our deepest, most intense feelings. It was freeing, and then it was just plain funny. We laughed and kicked back and downloaded each other on all the dirty details of everything we'd gone through the past couple days. Then, all of a sudden, we looked at each other with the same panic-stricken expression.

"They really aren't going to leave us alone, are they?" Cassie said.

"They have to be recording us," I agreed. "Somehow, they gotta be watching."

We bolted up from the sofa and ran around the suite looking for hidden cameras and mics. During the search, I found a drawer full of condoms, like a couple hundred of them. It was very optimistic, but given my status, I supposed they thought I'd maybe try to make up for lost time. Our frantic search complete, we met up in the bedroom, convinced that we were finally, truly, unbelievably, amazingly alone.

"I think it's really just us," I said.

"Yeah." She smiled.

I put my arms around Cass and pulled her close. "What do you want to do now?"

She smiled. "What do you want to do?"

What Happened in the Fantasy Suite

None of your business.

A Very Happy Short List

Start here.

1. Cass didn't know if she wanted to stay the night. She met with her producer beforehand to make sure she didn't have to if she wasn't comfortable. She was assured the decision was hers.

2. Cass was more in her head than I was about things a thoughtful person might and probably should consider before their first sleepover with someone. Did I snore? Did she snore? Did we both like the same side of the bed? Were pajamas necessary? How about toothpaste?

3. As it turned out, I heard the water while she was brushing her teeth and said, "You really leave the water running?"

4. The shower in the fantasy suite was all glass and right next to the bed, so there was no "Hey, I'm going to go take a shower. Be right

back." There was no doubt we were going to end up naked in front of each other.

5. We laughed so hard, and I saw Cassie in her most natural state: as an amazingly wonderful human being.

6. The next morning producers knocked on our door at 9:00 a.m. to shoot our last interview, a joint ITM. We didn't answer it. We weren't ready.

7. After we finally let them in, one of the producers asked: "So are you boyfriend and girlfriend now?" (We laughed.)

8. They wanted to know if we were thinking about getting engaged. (We laughed again. We weren't.)

9. They also asked if I lost anything overnight.

10. No one talks about their sex life unless they don't have one.

dark. The power went out. Was this a message from God? If so, what did it mean? Were we in the dark? Was it lights out, the end? Or was it the chance to flip a switch and see again with fresh eyes? Very quickly, though, we were like, who cares? We were in a strange house, in the middle of nowhere, and it was pitch-black.

This was scary stuff. It was time for me to man up! So Cass grabbed a humongous butcher knife and followed close behind me while I looked for the circuit breakers. I was ready to run. She was ready to pounce. A couple of times we got separated and I called out, "I'm coming around the corner. Don't stab me."

We didn't search long before I found the breaker box and reset the power. Problem solved. But then another one arose. It wasn't safe to be out in the countryside without any means of communication. What if there was a real emergency? We talked ourselves into a froth of what-ifs and ended up wanting our cell phones. They were packed away in our producers' rooms. I'd seen the envelope containing mine in Eileen's bag. Cass had seen the same with Martini. We went upstairs, rifled through their luggage, and snatched our phones. Within minutes, we were back downstairs, connected to the Wi-Fi, and FaceTiming with our parents.

Both of us had joyful catch-ups. We were in the process of returning our phones to their hiding places when Eileen and Martini arrived back in the house and said a loud, "Hello, you two." I sprinted downstairs to greet them, but Martini read my face and sensed something was up. He pushed past my feeble attempt to distract him with questions about their day and went straight upstairs and into his bedroom, where he caught Cassie standing over his open suitcase. Her confession was immediate and met with an amused chuckle.

"You guys can have your phones," he said. "It's not a big deal."

We had two months for re-entry into life back home. I spent Thanksgiving with my family in Colorado and then visited Cass

Happy Couple

No matter how long or short a relationship, every couple can look back on a moment after their first night together when they faced each other with a look of love and hope and more than a little fear of losing their hold over the TV remote and then ask, "What next?" For Cass and me, it was a nearby mansion in the hills above Mallorca, what was referred to as the Happy Couple house. We spent the next three days there and were instructed to enjoy ourselves.

Our producers, Eileen and Martini, accompanied us to the mansion. They took two of the bedrooms upstairs and left the large, opulent downstairs master bedroom for us. After sleeping in the next morning, they went out for the entire day and left the place to us. There were no cameras. No interviews. This was our time to be together. Cass and I did yoga, ate breakfast, and talked through the afternoon. By dinnertime, we were actually talking about what was next for us: Were we boyfriend and girlfriend? Would we get along once we were back in the real world? How were her parents going to react to us being together? And what about logistics? She lived in Huntington Beach and I was in Denver.

It was a lot to think about, and it was pretty darn serious for a brand-new couple. Then, all of a sudden, the whole house went and her family in Huntington Beach. She picked me up at the airport wearing a dark wig, a floppy hat, and sunglasses. Her family threw blankets over their windows for privacy. And we ensured this visit was lighter than the previous one by avoiding the serious topic of how we were going to keep seeing each other.

Forging a normal sense of coupledom was a challenge. After Christmas, almost all of my time was taken up with promotion of *The Bachelor.* I was in New York for *Dick Clark's New Year's Rockin' Eve* with Ryan Seacrest and Jenny McCarthy. Then it was back to LA for a three-hour live premiere party kicking off the new season, Monday, January 7. From then on, I traveled several times a week and stayed in touch with Cass with morning and late-night phone calls and text messages throughout the day.

We tried to see each other at least once a week and counted the days between the Happy Couple hideaways the show arranged for us, ensuring we had time together but always under the cover of secrecy. Our first was a cozy, two-bedroom Airbnb in the San Fernando Valley where we discovered the owners of the house were hiding out in the garage. Our next Happy Couple home was a mansion in LA, where I spent one entire day showering in each of the five different bathrooms while the show captured B-roll footage of me lathering up.

Cass was amused by the way my showers had caught on with fans. She exposed the truth about my showers: I was a messy clean freak. Yes, I relished my showers, but I left my towel and dirty clothes on the floor. Similarly, I made coffee in the morning but always left a little coffee puddle on the counter that needed wiping up. Cass was forgiving to a point. I crossed the line when I used her toothbrush. It grossed her out. I was like, what's the big deal? We make out, swap spit . . . what's the difference? To this day, I don't really understand the difference but I know never to do it again.

At the end of January, we celebrated my twenty-seventh birth-day in another Happy Couple home, where Cass surprised me with a re-creation of our Thailand date. I woke up in the morning and she led me into the backyard. I was blown away. There was a kid's pool with sand and seashells we'd brought back from our trip, a raft to represent our boat, and chilled champagne. Later, she even asked me again, "How do you not know by now?"

I laughed.

"I know! It's you! Game over!"

The game wasn't close to being over. Our happy-couple ren-dezvous were fun, but as Cass noted, they came with a price. We were prisoners in these palaces. We couldn't go outside, and we weren't supposed to have people over. Both of us were antsy, active people, so it was hard. She also said that under different circum-stances, like if we were dating, she would put on cute clothes and makeup. Instead, I got the natural, unadorned version with, as she put it, bad breath in the morning. I was ecstatic with any version of Cass.

As much as we wanted a normal life, it was impossible while the show was in season. The delay between the two of us in the present and what millions of people saw every Monday on TV worked against us in numerous ways, not the least of which was the emotional disconnect between then and the present. The fourth episode—my date with Caelynn in Singapore—was particularly hard on Cass. Seeing me connect with other girls upset her.

"I feel like this is supposed to be our love story," she said. "Nobody gets to see it. Our first kiss never aired. Nobody knows who I am. And in a few weeks, they're just going to see me break your heart."

It got better as the show progressed, but Cassie had it much harder than me. People recognized her and made comments like, "Hannah's amazing, isn't she?" and "Caelynn's so pretty. Don't you love her?" They didn't know Cass and I were together. I reached out to Becca and asked her to speak with Cassie. The four of us actually got on the phone together—me and Cass and Becca and Garrett—and Becca said, "You guys know what you have. Don't worry about what's going on in the show or what people are saying about you. Focus on the truth and growing your relationship."

Her advice helped. We watched the Thailand episode with Cassie's family in Huntington Beach. It wasn't too uncomfortable with all of them watching us make out. But I swear I saw Cassie's dad playing with a pocketknife through much of our date. She disagrees. We assured them we didn't just make out in the water. We talked, too. They were good sports and thank goodness no one took it too seriously.

Cassie watched hometowns at a restaurant with her family. I joined them the next week for our breakup in Portugal. I couldn't have picked a tougher episode. The fence jump was heavily promoted and anticipation of some kind of drama was intense. It was all over TV, the Internet, magazines in the grocery store. Cassie's parents opened their door to family and friends, including her brother's girlfriend's family. I cringed the full hour. It was all so raw and agonizing and hard to relive, and more than slightly embarrassing to share with everyone.

But no one else seemed to have a problem, especially Cassie's dad. In the part when I told Cassie that he hadn't given me his blessing, Matt actually paused the TV and said, "Did you really think I was going to give you permission after just six weeks?" Every head in the room turned in my direction. I shrugged. It was actually kind of funny.

At least I had the benefit of knowing that Cass was sitting next to me and holding my hand. She was much better than me at paying attention to what really mattered. At the end of the episode, I said, "Thank God," and shut my eyes. My phone and social media blew up with people supporting Cassie and others who were curious why I was into someone who didn't want to be with me. I heard from a slew of pro football players from across the league.

"Too bad I don't have my sports agent anymore," I tweeted. "This is the most traction I've ever gotten in the NFL."

The live finale in March 2019 didn't come fast enough. Three months of hiding out and keeping our relationship under wraps was finally over. In the afternoon, we limoed to Hollywood to tape an appearance on Jimmy Kimmel for later that night. Technically, his audience was the first to see Cass and me together. I laughed as Jimmy introduced me as "a twenty-seven-year-old virgin who loved his virginity so much he wanted to go on national television to lose it." Cassie liked hearing that Jimmy's wife knew from the beginning that we'd end up together. "So what happened in that fantasy suite?" he joked.

After Kimmel, Cass and I split up and got ready for the three-hour live finale. On my way to the studio, something strange and wonderful happened. While stopped at a red light, my car was suddenly overtaken by thousands of painted lady butterflies. At the time, an estimated one billion painted lady butterflies were migrating from Mexico to the Pacific Northwest, and Los Angeles was like a waystation. For a moment, all of them appeared to be surrounding my car. The sight was surreal. I thought of Cassie and how she gave me a box of butterflies when I met her on the very first night. I sent her a picture and wrote, "We were meant to be."

Several hours later, our couplehood was a secret no more. The moment people on both coasts knew Cass and I were together, we made it official with postings on our respective Instagram pages. I told my grandma that's what kids these days do. Both of us were immediately flooded with text messages, calls, tweets, and comments on Instagram. Cass said it seemed like everyone she'd never known or met wanted to congratulate her. People were so happy for us. It was a great feeling and almost too much to process.

Indeed, the two of us still had so much to figure out on our own, but oh man, was it ever obvious that people love a good love story.

And word was only starting to get out. With producers literally pushing us out of the studio doors in order to make our flight, a black SUV whisked us to the airport, onto the tarmac, and right up to a Delta jet headed to New York, where we had a week of interviews ahead of us, starting early the next day with *Good Morning America*.

Exhausted, Cass and I fell asleep together in my first-class cubicle. In what seemed like a blink, we were in New York. We changed clothes in the bathrooms at JFK and drove straight to *GMA* and then did nonstop interviews afterward. As I went to sleep that night, I heard myself from earlier as if on a loop. Yes, we were together, and no, we weren't engaged, and yeah, it seemed like we were boyfriend and girlfriend now. Cassie was quizzed about her decision to break up with me and why she couldn't seem to "get there" with me. When asked about the future, we shrugged and said we had to figure that out.

Actually, our plans were fairly straightforward: we wanted to get to know each other better. I moved to Los Angeles to be closer to Cass. She got an apartment with her sister in West Hollywood and worked to juggle graduate school, an internship, her family, and a persistent, pestering, sometimes annoying boyfriend—me.

Simple, quiet time together, like going to the beach, hiking, or doing yoga, became the moments we cherished most of all. Not surprisingly, those were also the moments we needed. We traveled to New York together, walked red carpets at events, and posed for the cover of *People* magazine, but none of that gave us the time we needed to get to know each other. As Cass periodically reminded me, we'd missed a step in our relationship—the part where you date and flirt, make plans, discover cute things about each other, anticipate going out to dinner, get stuck in traffic, check out each other's playlists, and gradually get to know each other . . . in other words, the fun stuff, the stuff that creates the foundation a relationship needs if it's going to go the distance.

I knew she was right. I wondered how she knew and I didn't. I don't want to start any wars with this statement, but I'm sure it had something to do with the wisdom, insight, and intelligence that women have and men don't.

As I discovered, there really was something special, fun, and necessary about taking it slow, which was the point Cassie's dad made during hometowns, and it's the tact we endeavored to take. We called each other. We made dates. I went over to her place. She stopped by mine. I learned that I didn't have to spend every waking minute with her, and she enjoyed missing me on the days we didn't spend together. We put friendship first and began to build a real relationship, not one made for TV.

I learned Cass likes scary movies and chocolate ice cream. She discovered I favor action thrillers and a spoonful of peanut butter and honey. She likes cream in her coffee, and I take mine black with sweetener. At restaurants, she looks at the menu without ever making up her mind and I end up ordering for both of us—and usually way too much. She likes wearing sweatpants as much as I do. I order sangria, and Cass likes a cold beer. My dad loves her for that—she's like the son he never had (with apologies to my brother, Connor).

Cass hates to shop, and I've made her more bougey and materialistic than she ever imagined. She says I'm an awful driver, which I guess is why I like the self-driving feature on my Tesla. Cass, by the way, drives a 2005 Honda CR-V she's named Duke. Why Duke? It sounds beachy to her. I pass out as soon as my head hits the pillow, and she likes to read before falling asleep. I often wake up with a

Kindle next to me. She hugs my dog, Sniper, and I let her kittens claw on my sweatshirt while we watch TV.

It's been good, and when it hasn't, it's been a learning experience. In April, I joined Cassie and her family for their annual pilgrimage to the Stagecoach country music festival, a three-day jamboree featuring Luke Bryan, Jason Aldean, and other top acts in Indio. For years, her family pulled up in an RV, picnicked, and enjoyed the headliners from the general-admission section. Eager to impress and ingratiate myself, I used my new celebrity clout to rent a house and get VIP passes and perks that I thought would make it even more memorable. It didn't—and it's probably best to leave it at that.

In August, Cass and I broke up. I know, I know, it hit me like that, too—hard. Nothing big happened between us as much as little things built up until they became big. It boiled down to me wanting to get engaged, wanting to set a timeline, and simply putting too much pressure on her when, in reality, none was needed. I wanted more. She wanted me to relax and smell the roses. In other words, don't push. Don't pressure. I interpreted that to mean she didn't care about our relationship.

That night will not go down as one of our best, and Cass left my house in tears. Fourteen hours later, she knocked on my door and we talked the rest of the day and into the night. In the process, other issues came out. She pledged to help me have a better relationship with her family, and I promised to chill. It was one of those things that new couples have to go through to discover and develop the resiliency needed in relationships. We were continuing to learn communication, understanding, compromise, and a willingness to forgive. Also just how much we really, truly wanted to be together.

The next time a problem arose, we were able to handle it. It was October, and Cass was about to leave on a trip to Paris with her mom when stories that we were breaking up appeared on several Bachelor Nation threads on the Internet. Our relationship was perfectly intact, but some of the details were accurate enough to make us feel betrayed by someone close to us. Instead of letting this spiral into an issue about trust, we addressed the problem together and emerged stronger and closer because of it.

Navigating a relationship in public is a unique experience. We can't have an argument in a restaurant without someone posting a photo that we are breaking up. Paparazzi follow us at the grocery store, the coffee shop, and the beach. Almost anything we share on social media triggers comments and speculation: people get angry that we're together, others criticize the way we look and what we wear, and some even root for a breakup. But all of that pales compared to having millions of people rooting for you. That's our reality. They want Cass and me to be happy. They know how hard it is to meet the right person and get to the next step. They want the love to be real and to last. And so do we. The best stories are love stories, and we're trying to write our own happily ever after.

This is something I hoped might happen when I got involved with *The Bachelorette*. It was a fantasy when I began to imagine becoming the Bachelor. Who does that? I grew up surrounded by cornfields and family. I thought I'd meet someone in high school or my hometown and never leave. I never expected to meet someone like Cass and fall in love the way I did. I prayed someone special like her would come into my life. But how? I was a broken-down football player living in my dad's basement in Colorado. What was I going to do, go on one of those TV dating programs? Who do any of us know that goes on TV and meets the person who could be their forever?

I turned out to be that guy. I opened up my love life to TV. I took what crushed me in high school and college, along with all the insecurities that went into making me a twentysomething-year-old virgin and put them out where the whole world could see them. Instead of destroying me, I got stronger, more self-confident, and maybe, hopefully, a little wiser. Thinking about it right now, all I did was admit that I was human. I was an all-American former pro football player who didn't have all the answers.

I tell people: Be who you are, and if you aren't sure, don't be afraid to try things that will help you figure it out. Don't worry about what other people think. If they give you trouble, come find me and we'll talk to them.

Like so many people my age, and maybe like you, I am a mix of contradictions as I try to figure out where I fit in. I can be tough one day and cry the next. I can get angry, but I can be vulnerable, too. My mood changes daily. I make mistakes. I am not afraid to try new things. I want to be successful. But I find the most meaning when I help other people. There's something about giving selflessly that makes me my best self.

Going on *The Bachelor* brought a lot to me—some good, some bad, and some I'll never be able to figure out. I went looking for love and found out more about myself than I imagined, and in the process I met a twenty-four-year-old speech pathologist who gave me a box of butterflies. Now, a year later, she still gives me butterflies every time I see her. I do my best to make her feel the same way about me. Will we always be together? I hope so. We want our happily ever after. We are working at it. But I can't see into the future. I focus instead on loving Cassie today and tomorrow, and knowing that love comes back to me tenfold. If that continues, we will have our forever.

She once asked me, "How do you not know?"

There are so many things in this life that are impossible to know.

But when the question concerns love, you do know.

I did.

I still do.

I may be unsure where it will take me, but I know it's taking me on an incredible journey.

Acknowledgments

I am smiling as I sit at my dining room table, writing this section. The reason for my good mood should be obvious. I get to say thank you to people who have been incredibly helpful and important to me throughout my life—and to all of you who I have yet to meet personally but am aware that you're out there rooting for me.

Bachelor Nation, you gave me the reason to write a book. We connected when I was on *The Bachelorette*, and you supported me all the way through my journey as the Bachelor. My life has never been the same because of those shows—and all of you. Let's keep it going. Shoot me a text at (310) 299-9264. Let's talk.

This book is also about my experiences beyond TV, those spanning my twenty-eight years on this planet. It's a relatively short amount of time, but it's an entire lifetime to me. It has been filled with some of the most incredible people I can imagine, including my rocks Mike Zimmer, Coach Nowinsky, Sam Ryan, Colin Ash, and Kyle Donarski. Thanks for always being there for me.

As for this book itself, I want all those involved to know how much I appreciate your help in making it really happen, starting with my editor, Natasha Simons, the first to believe that I could be an author, that I had a story to tell, and for helping me tell it.

Natasha, though you're on one coast and I'm on the other, please accept a rose from me.

I have a few additional roses for the talented design, marketing, and PR team at Gallery Books who transformed my typewritten pages into a real book that would blow the mind of every teacher I ever had in school. Thank you Sally Marvin, Jennifer Robinson, John Vairo, Abby Zidle, Samantha Hoback, and the boss, Jennifer Bergstrom. Also, special thank you to Maggie Loughran for your invaluable assistance in organizing drafts and photos, keeping facts straight, the deadlines tight, and the emails friendly. You get a rose, too.

I also want to offer a shout-out to my team at Artists First, Randi Michel and Cait Lang. Your advice and guidance this past year has been greatly appreciated.

Then Dan Strone, the Chris Harrison of my literary agency, Trident Media Group. Thank you for opening the door to this world and shepherding me through it. Also for introducing me to Todd Gold, who was an even better dude than you said. He gets a rose, too. Trident's Rosemary LoVoi deserves her own thank-you for all her assistance—and the final rose I'm handing out in this section. I remember my first visit to the Trident Media Group offices and meeting everyone there. Let's do it again soon.

Now the personal stuff. This book wouldn't exist without the Randolph family. Thank you for your patience, love, and sense of humor, and for allowing me to come into your house and flip your lives upside down. I love sleeping on the third-story couch. Seriously. It's comfy—and that's because of the warmth all of you have shared with me.

And my family. My heart is full as I think about all of you. I have to start by acknowledging the person in my life who has been there for me, and at my feet, for the longest, and reacted to everything with unconditional love—my dog, Sniper. And then Mom and Dad, who not only created me but shaped me into the person I am today and gave me the tools and desire and courage to continue to grow. I end every phone call with you by saying, "I love you," and I mean it. Thank you to my bonus mom and my bonus dad for the way you entered my life and enhanced it and continue to make it better and brighter.

Big hugs to my brother, Connor, and all of my bonus siblings; please know that, as I have always told you, I am always right, and when Mom and Dad say, "Why can't you be more like your older brother Colton?" they mean it. And to my aunts Shannon, Stephanie, and Sherrie, thank you for all summers we spent together and for helping to raise me. And Nana and Papa—I love you and I'm looking forward to beating you in our next card game (and hearing your thoughts on this book). And Papa Fish and Nancy— thank you for being so supportive over the years. Love you guys.

Cass—there's nothing I can possibly say here that I haven't said in this book or on national TV, and the stuff I say to you in private will remain, for a change, just between us. However, just so everyone knows, you make my world go 'round. I love you.